Where's that Poem?

Where's that Poem?

AN INDEX OF
POEMS FOR CHILDREN

Arranged by Subject, with
a Bibliography of Books of Poetry
and an Introduction on the
Teaching of Poetry

by HELEN MORRIS
Senior Lecturer in English
HOMERTON COLLEGE, CAMBRIDGE

OXFORD · BASIL BLACKWELL ·

© Basil Blackwell 1967

Reprinted January 1970

631 10100 4

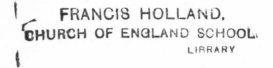
Printed in Great Britain by
Alden & Mowbray Ltd
at the Alden Press, Oxford
and bound by
the Kemp Hall Bindery

to NORAH BARTLETT

for much generous advice, encouragement
and technical instruction,
my most grateful and affectionate thanks

Contents

Foreword

This index was begun because I was so often asked by students in a College of Education 'Do you remember that poem about . . . about nightingales, or nightmares, or Noah, or noise? And where can I find it?' I began to list poems and keep references, and the list became this book, which I hope may be useful to everyone who teaches poetry.

The poems have been chosen with children of approximately seven to fifteen years old in mind. Children of five and six are usually best suited by nursery rhymes and jingles, of which there are several admirable collections—Puffin Book of Nursery Rhymes, Oxford Nursery Rhyme Book, listed as PUF.N.R. and OX.N.R. in the book-list at the end of this book. Still, many poems mentioned here can be read to and with even these youngest children, in the infant school. The teacher of children of fifteen and upwards will naturally use a wide selection of adult poetry to suit both his own tastes and that of each of his classes. But how artificial such divisions are! Much great poetry can be apprehended (admittedly at different levels) both by small children and by adults; parts of *The Ancient Mariner*, some of Blake's songs and some of Robert Frost's lyrics are cases in point.

To classify poems as suitable for a particular age-group is to err in two ways: it is to expect a poem to speak exclusively to children at a certain stage of development, and to assume that children of a certain age are all at the same stage of poetic education and appreciation. The appreciation of poetry to any sophisticated degree has to be learnt, as much as the appreciation of music or art. Even though certain poems—like certain tunes and paintings —may at first hearing or sight be simple and obvious enough to appeal to the uneducated, yet it is the teacher's business to foster appreciation of more difficult poetry by a really careful and sensitive choice of poems for each individual class—and, if possible, for each individual child. Some teachers invariably demand that every child turn to the same poem in the one available anthology, and that the whole class concentrate on that poem. But—once poetry is established as worth reading, because interesting or even exciting—each child should be given time to browse in different books of poems, while the teacher circulates with quiet words of individual guidance. Thus the child learns to choose for himself a poem that has something to say to him personally, to copy the poem into his personal anthology, or to read it aloud to the teacher or to the class. To say that a particular poem is suitable for a child of a particular age is to try to cram every child into a teacher-designed and teacher-enforced scheme of development which bears no resemblance to real personal, individual growth.

Many poems which, taken complete, are obviously unsuitable for children, yet have a few lines a teacher longs to use—for instance, Edward Thomas's *Aspens* (see ASPENS), and several poems by Andrew Young. I have indexed a few of such poems, because I take it for granted that anyone using this book will do so with discrimination, picking and choosing the appropriate material for his particular class.

Since grouping by age seems impracticable, the poems have been grouped under subject-headings, with ample cross-reference. A few 'kinds', such as limericks and riddles, are included (see p. xxxv) simply because this seemed useful. Carols, ballads and nursery-rhymes are not listed as such, but many appear under subject-headings. Some songs by Shakespeare are here, and often children also enjoy snatches from the plays; but very few of the latter have been included, lest the work swell beyond all bounds. Every teacher must have a fund of his own favourite passages, a line or two to quote at an appropriate moment; children may remember these, though not wholly understanding them, and grow later to full appreciation.

Sometimes a group of poems on the same subject is divided

into two sections 'Lyric and Descriptive' and 'Narrative', so
that the teacher looking for a few vivid lines will not find a long
story, and vice versa.

Reference is given to a wide variety of sources—pp. 273 to 300
list 141 titles, comprising 197 volumes—since different schools
possess different books. It is hoped that every teacher will procure
as many different books of poetry as possible, and thus give
every child the opportunity of browsing widely. It is far better
to have five copies of each of six books than thirty of the same
book, in the classroom library. In the index, each book is indicated by a symbol—a group of letters which indicate its title if an
anthology, and its author if it is by a single poet. These symbols are explained on p. 273 and arranged alphabetically on
pp. 273 to 300 for easy reference and identification, with
necessary particulars about each book. A few words of com-
ment on each may, I hope, assist the teacher who is engaged
in building up a library of books of poetry for personal use
or for the class, to decide whether any particular book is
worth closer inspection.

Most of the books used are anthologies designed for children,
and there are a few useful adult anthologies. I wished to include
certain poems which do not appear in any of the anthologies cited
so I have given some references to books by single authors,
among them Blake, Frost, Graves, Kipling and Yeats, hoping
that this will encourage other teachers to search adult poetry for
poems which their classes will enjoy.

The experienced teacher will have a hundred individual ways
of dealing with as many poems, but the student or the novice may
find it useful to have some suggestions about introducing poetry
to children, and these precede the actual index.

I should like to thank those of my friends who have helped me
in the confusing work of compilation, particularly Judith
Broadhead, Bridget Hill, Elizabeth Pestell and Jacqueline Webb.
Norah Bartlett has at every stage put at my disposal her wide

knowledge of books and her bibliographical expertise; her help has been invaluable.

The responsibility for the choice of poems is entirely mine: no poem is included that I would not, in particular circumstances, be happy to offer to a class.

Giving Poems to Children

This index is by no means comprehensive, but highly selective and personal. No one person can choose poems for another to teach with any *certainty* of success—though many poems are widely popular with the majority of teachers and of children. No teacher should ever give a class a poem, however much other teachers recommend it, unless he himself receives genuine pleasure from it. Better not to teach poetry at all than to teach it without enjoyment, for the wrong kind of poetry-teaching can awaken such resentment in a child that he never again will read a poem for pleasure.

A moment's consideration of the perpetual chanting and singing going on in the playground of any school (see I. and P. Opie, *Language and Lore of Schoolchildren* and James Ritchie, *The Singing Street*) should convince us that children have an innate delight in rhyme and rhythm. What happens to that delight, in the course of schooling, to make so many secondary classes literally groan when the word poetry is mentioned? The teacher of poetry should not have to create an appetite for it, but merely to educate the appetite that every child originally possesses.

Children allergic to 'poetry' are often delighted when it is suggested that they should consider 'folk-song'. The teacher, like St. Paul, must use 'any manner of means' to convey his message, and should be willing to cash in—though always with discrimination—on the recent boom in folk-song and folk-singers. Many folk-songs, sea shanties and freedom songs from the United States are included here under appropriate headings, and it need not be emphasized that folk-songs—for instance *Lord Randall* (see MURDER) or *O Waly Waly* (see LOVE SONGS (UNHAPPY))—can have true poetic quality. If the teacher can learn a few guitar chords and encourage actual singing, so much the better (see pp. xxv, xxxii).

Full advantage should be taken of recorded poetry; several anthologies have accompanying records, and many of these readings are arresting and delightful. There is now a wide variety of recorded poetry, much of it suitable for children, read both by actors and by poets. A poem by Robert Frost, for instance, gains immeasurably from a hearing of it in the voice of the poet himself. The teacher should also if possible use a tape recorder to collect striking performances by friends, for use in his classroom, and also to record the most successful readings by children, particularly of their own work. There can be real eagerness to learn by heart poems which, when perfected, are to be recorded.

It is obvious that it must be made as easy and pleasant as possible for each child to comprehend the poems the teacher presents. But how often a teacher merely reads a poem aloud, not particularly well, and then expects the children to understand it and be able to answer questions about it. How many adults could do this, without much practice in listening—and much intelligence? Ideally, each child should have a copy of the poem in front of him or (as Professor I. A. Richards preferred at Harvard) the poem can be clearly set out on a screen, blackboard or poster, so that the whole class is reading from the same copy. In the latter case the teacher must himself go to the farthest part of the room and make sure that the poem is clearly legible even from that point.

Choosing Poems for Children

Children should meet poems of every imaginable kind: poems long and short; poems lyric, narrative, descriptive, satiric, didactic; poems serious and comic; poems and verses about the trivia of everyday life and poems about love and death. There is only one test: each must be good of its own kind. The narrative must hold the listener; the poem of sentiment must not degenerate into sentimentality; 'even a limerick', said W. H. Auden, 'ought to be something a man of honour, awaiting death from cancer or a firing squad, could read without contempt'.

Good poetry is strong and vital—often tough—not feeble, pretty and lifeless. The limp and anaemic 'children's verse' of some older anthologies must be avoided like the plague—and so, I think, should some of the 'sick' poems which are included by a few anthologists over-anxious to be 'modern'. This is not a matter of subject. Battle, murder and sudden death are a part of life, and a part of poetry, and not to be kept from even the youngest; it is a question of tone, and of the outlook and approach of the poet.

In a sense, a chief purpose of education is to teach discrimination, to teach children to recognise the difference between the best and the worst, and then the difference between the best and the second-best, in every sphere of human activity. The teacher of poetry must himself be able to discriminate finely: a hard task, but one which grows more possible with practice.

Using the Poems

Special poetry lessons—that is, periods specifically devoted to the enjoyment of poetry—may of course be given, and can be eagerly looked forward to by the class. But many teachers now prefer to include a certain amount of poetry in almost every English lesson, and to devote a substantial amount of time to poetry in the general session of 'Reading by the Teacher' which is so strongly advocated nowadays. For the younger children several short periods are better than a long one, and a variety both of poems and of activities can be offered in each period— listening, reading silently, reading aloud, alone or in chorus, acting and miming, copying favourite poems into individual folders, illustrating poems. With all children, but particularly with juniors, the minimum of analysis or explanation should be given—the poem's the thing.

Two groups of students, one at a college of education, the other at a centre for further education, recently wrote about their personal experiences of being taught poetry. Almost all remarked that while they had enjoyed poetry lessons in the junior school, they had much disliked them in the secondary school, whether grammar, comprehensive or secondary modern. The repeated grounds of complaint were that the poems were over-elaborately analysed, 'torn to bits', 'chewed to pieces', that discussion was rarely permitted, and that when it was the teacher almost invariably insisted that the poem had only one 'correct' meaning or explanation—the one supplied by the teacher. Surely in secondary classes free discussion should be encouraged. Unless gross misunderstanding is apparent, alternative views of the poem's meaning and significance should be invited and willingly considered, and left for each pupil to mull over later by himself.

Sometimes one particular poem can be closely explored—but

never to boredom—or a group of poems, carefully chosen to illuminate one another, can be presented. Here this index may be helpful in suggesting a group of poems on one, or similar, subjects. These may be treated in different ways by poets contemporary with one another, or sometimes in the same way by poets living hundreds of years apart. What matters in any poem is the total experience it provides, and sharing this experience should delight us, enlarge our understanding and truly educate us.

It cannot be too strongly emphasized that no single standard approach to 'a poem', as such, is possible. Students in some colleges of education have actually been asked to choose and prepare a poem for a class, 'asking eight questions'. But the number of questions put to the class by the teacher—if any are necessary—must be appropriate to the particular poem which has been introduced; they must be very carefully framed, and modified according to the response of the class to the poem.

Here one can only plead that the poetry lesson should aim at a true comprehension of the total experience of the poem, and must never degenerate into a kind of exercise in 'comprehension' in the exercise book or examination sense. Questions must never be posed which can be answered by a single word or line lifted uncomprehendingly from the poem. The Jumblies 'went to sea in a sieve'. The question, 'What did they go to sea in?' will elicit from even a slow child the answer, 'They went to sea in a sieve'. Some teachers will tick it, and pass on. But once, on questioning a class almost all of whom had answered this question 'correctly', I found that a large proportion of the children had but the vaguest idea of what a sieve actually was—'Is it some kind of boat, miss?'—and had therefore entirely missed Lear's point.

Difficult or unfamiliar words must perhaps be explained, and this can sometimes be done best in discussion before the poem is read, but unsuitable questions can easily kill the poem stone dead. I take an actual example.

The class were reading *The Listeners* (see MYSTERY) and

the homework had been to read it carefully and to learn the first twelve lines by heart.

> *'Is there anybody there?' said the Traveller,*
> *Knocking on the moonlit door;*
> *And his horse in the silence champed the grasses*
> *Of the forest's ferny floor: . . .*

The lesson began with the command to put away their poetry books, then each child was given a sheet of paper, and told to numbers its lines from 1 to 20. Twenty questions were then read:

1. Who came to the door?
2. What did he say?
3. What was he doing?
4. What did his horse do?

and so on.

Equally deadly for most children is the study of form, or of figurative language, for their own sakes. Of course it is essential to establish the rhythmical nature of poetry, and one of the best ways is to show how song has been used to help a man to do a a job—to row a boat, to chop down a tree, or to bounce a ball in the playground. Kay Melzi recounts (*Art in the Primary School*, Blackwell 1967) how a form of backward eight-year-olds were discovered helping themselves to sew by chanting as they slowly pushed their needles,

> *'In, out,*
> *A Bottle of Stout';*

as they got faster, they changed it to

> *'Out, in,*
> *A Bottle of Gin'.*

'Michael, row the boat ashore' (see ROWING), and the sea shanties which use different rhythms for different tasks, are excellent examples of grown-ups doing the same thing. Children readily recognize train rhythms in, for instance, *From a Railway*

Carriage or parts of *Night Mail* (see TRAINS); more readily still in repetition of the American nonsense phrase, 'Hiney menoosh, hiney menoosh'. The 'reversed menu' which imitates the engine getting under way is always popular:

> *Coffee, coffee, coffee, coffee;*
> *Cheese and biscuits—*   (repeated thrice)
> *Fruit and custard—*   (repeated thrice)
> *Fish and chips—*   (repeated thrice)
> *Soo . . . oup.*   (once only)

Children can experience and differentiate between the galloping rhythm of Browning's *'How they brought the good news'* (see RIDING), the dancing movement of de la Mare's *Off the Ground* (see DANCING), the smooth rocking of a lullaby (see LULLA-BIES) and the tumultuous rushing of Southey's *Cataract at Lodore* (see WATERFALLS). But talk of scansion, of iambs and dactyls, is usually merely confusing.

So is a pedantic approach to figures of speech. To read a poem and then to demand that each child pick out a simile, or count the number of metaphors in verse three, is useless. What is valuable is to show how by comparing one thing with another we may get a new insight into some familiar object or experience. Blake's children flowing into 'the high dome of Paul's' 'like Thames' waters'; Christina Rossetti's moon 'tired . . . pale . . . within her misty, misty veil'; James Reeves' sea like 'a hungry dog'; Hardy's woodmen as executioners, or his wind which 'raved round the land'; Philip Larkin's 'toad, work'; these and a thousand other images can give insight and lead the children to make their own lively, original and vivid comparisons, a thousand miles distant from the stock exercises still found: 'Complete the following: As black as . . . ' with the one fixed answer, 'Soot'.

Surely the whole point of encouraging children to make comparisons is not to teach them to repeat the stale clichés which are still enumerated in books of English exercises and in certain examinations, but to encourage them to draw from their own observation and experience images as personal, as original and as telling as possible. One class doubted whether Tennyson's 'black as ash-buds in March' was valid. A boy remembered the discussion, and when March arrived he brought in an ash-twig to prove the poet accurate. The children were encouraged to suggest their own comparisons, and one (looking at the teacher's fashionably-thickly-clad legs) suggested 'black as teacher's stockings'. This was in fact far more meaningful for the class than 'soot', for many of them lived in homes with no open fires.

Everyday experience should provide the material for poetic images created by children themselves. Leaves in autumn twirling 'like clothes in a spin-drier', a man who suddenly changed the subject of conversation 'switching to another channel', finger-marks on the icing of a cake looking like the marks of stiletto heels on linoleum—all these are expressive and have validity, because they arise from immediate personal experience.

But in an eleven-plus examination one child was given no marks for 'smooth as a baby's bottom' (though it is a proverbial saying in some parts of England, and he may well have known its truth from experience); the 'correct' answer was 'smooth as satin', a substance he had probably never felt.

Whole new worlds can be created through poetic imagery. De la Mare's *The Fly* (see FLIES) can release the child's imagination and truly establish the conception of relative scale, so hard to convey as an abstraction.

> *How large unto the tiny fly*
> *Must little things appear!*
> *A rosebud like a feather-bed,*
> *Its prickle like a spear.*

After some discussion of the complete poem a group of children suggested further comparisons from the fly's standpoint, and then wrote compositions on the human world as seen by a giant —a giant who used a clothes-prop for a tooth-pick, stole sheets off the clothes-line for pocket-handkerchiefs, tied barges to his feet as sandals, and caused havoc by sitting down on Waterloo Bridge to dangle his feet in the Thames. These are of course lively but grotesque images, quoted merely to demonstrate how the imagination can be stirred by a poem.

I have heard a student teacher read Stevenson's *Windy Nights* (see WIND)—

> *All in the night when the stars are out,*
> *Why does he gallop and gallop about?*—

and then ask the class to imagine what sort of a man would gallop about at night. She accepted happily 'messengers' and 'highwaymen'; after a momentary hesitation she accepted 'ghosts', and then set the children to illustrate the poem. I was sad to see a small boy rebuked for drawing only a lonely, empty road with storm-tossed trees—for surely he (surpassing his teacher in understanding) realised that the ghostly horseman was the immaterial wind itself.

Poems should sometimes be chosen with relevance to an immediate experience of the children. On a day of particularly striking weather—after a sudden snowstorm, for instance, when the children will have wakened to find the light mysteriously different, and the whole aspect of the world outside quite altered overnight—it may be worth scrapping, or postponing, a prepared poetry lesson, and choosing from the index a few poems which express this experience. These may well stimulate the children to write of their own reactions (see p. xxii). It is well to choose more than one poem, to show that snow, or the first day of spring, or fog, can be described and experienced in very different ways.

2. CHILDREN'S PARTICIPATION

It is hardly necessary to say that the children should participate as much as possible in the lesson, poor readers as well as skilful ones.

But a poor reader stumbling his semi-audible way through a poem will be at best boring, and at worst will permanently wreck the poem for the rest of the class. It is best to have some-times the whole class, sometimes groups of children in turn, reading aloud together. The teacher will at first lead the speakers, and always be ready to help with a difficult word or an unex-pected accentuation, so that the reading can go forward uninterruptedly.

Many poems (see SPIRITUALS, SEA SHANTIES) fall naturally into verse and chorus, which can be read by different sections of the class alternately, as can the poems in QUES-TION & ANSWER and BALLADS, RIDDLING. The divisions must always be meaningful; to read a single line each round the class, or to have the two halves of the class reading alternate lines —and this is still done in some schools—can turn a poem to nonsense. Where a poem is a unity, it must be perceived as an integrated whole.

It was encouraging to see a class of rather slow nine-year-olds, who had been thoroughly unenthusiastic about poetry, eagerly waiting for the right moment to exclaim 'The Akond of Swat!' (see NONSENSE (LEAR)) at the end of each verse of that admirable poem, which their teacher was reading with *brio*. She proceeded to Eleanor Farjeon's *Hannibal* (see HANNIBAL). Each row of children became a part of the army—'countrymen and townmen' or 'black men and brown men'. There was some competition to be 'his lions and his elephants' and everyone joined in the rousing *finale*:

> *And* that's *why Hannibal, Hannibal, Hannibal,*
> *Hannibal crossed the Alps!*

As confidence in their own power of reading aloud grows, and self-consciousness diminishes through continual practice, individual voices can be used, and children can, in turn, during the term, read favourite poems aloud to all the class. It is well worth having the individual reader come to the front of the class and face his, or her, audience. The teacher should not stand beside him, but go to the back of the room—to make sure that everyone can hear—and from there can signal approbation and encouragement to the reader, more or less unobserved. This lesson should never be made an occasion for stern reproof or reproach—the whole idea is to give children confidence in their powers of choice, of exposition and of expression. For as confidence grows, it can become a habit that the child reading a poem he has chosen will preface it with a few words explaining or justifying the choice. Some choices the teacher may privately deplore—but not publicly. He should merely find better poems in some way related, and give them in the ordinary course of the lessons.

If the children are to read and choose freely from the books of poetry in the classroom, it is obviously extremely important that these should be the very best available. As regards poetry, as well as much else, Juvenal's 1900-year-old maxim is still true: *Maxima debetur puero reverentia:* the greatest respect is due to a child. Only the best is good enough for children.

3. MIME, DRAMA AND DANCE

From reading aloud it is a short step to acting. Drama is outside the scope of this preface, but informal, spontaneous acting inspired by the reading of narrative verse, or of a poem with a dramatic flavour, can be a frequent and enjoyable part of poetry lessons. It is not easy to act while holding a book, yet children may want to act out straight away a poem that takes their fancy, before there has been time to memorize it. Often the solution is for one group to mime while other children read aloud. Ballads, for instance *Sir Patrick Spens* (see SHIPWRECKS) or *The Wife of Usher's Well* (see GHOSTS), lend themselves particularly well to reading in parts and to mimed actions, and so does *The Daniel Jazz* (see DANIEL) (see also p. xxx).

Teachers of Modern Dance, too, use poems for their rhythm, their story, their atmosphere or sometimes for the onomatopoeic quality of their words. Southey's *Cataract of Lodore* (see WATER-FALLS), the different rhythms of Masefield's *Cargoes* (see SHIPS), the atmosphere created by the first lines of de la Mare's *Silver* (see NIGHT)—these are a few examples which have evoked expressive movement.

4. ENCOURAGING CHILDREN'S WRITING

It is a vexed question whether it is useful to read poems to children just before the children attempt to write poems themselves. Often only very second-hand and feebly imitative work results, and on the whole it seems better to keep the reading and the writing of poetry as separate activities. We are not here, of course, considering the abler, older child who can find both parody and imitation delightful and rewarding exercises (see PARODY).

It is astounding how the reading of a poem can impose itself on the children's writing and exert a profound influence, good or bad. One class of ten-year-olds enjoyed Nashe's *Spring* (see SPRING) so much that their poems for months afterwards had refrains recalling his 'Cuckoo, jug-jug, pu-we, towitta woo', though applied to such disparate things as trains ('Chuff, Chuff, chuff-chuff-chuff, chooooooo') and pigs ('Grunt, grunt, huck huck, ha-uch').

Eleanor Farjeon's *Cat*! (see CATS) produced this variation by a nine-year-old girl, written at home in her own time:

> *Scat Cat!*
> *Run after the rat*
> *Scat Cat!*
> *You may run*
> *And you may spring*
> *But Scat Cat!*
> *Run after the rat*
> *Scat Cat!*
> *You may hiss*

And you may howl
But Scat Cat!
Run after the rat
Scat Cat!

Under PARODY will be found a poem by an older schoolboy, *Lessons on Maths*, worth reading for its own sake, and also as being inspired by *Lessons of the War: the Naming of Parts* (see WARS: 1939–45: TRAINING).

Children can complete poems they regard as unfinished— given the first verses only of some ballad, they can tell the rest of the story to their own fancy. And one class enjoyed reading Kipling's *The King* (see ROMANCE) in which cave-men, soldiers and skippers in turn deplore the passing of the old 'romantic' ways; the class completed it by showing how the allegedly unromantic steam engine—when replaced by diesels— is nowadays regarded with fond sentiment.

For many children, a picture will evoke a poem. A seven-year-old, looking at a picture, wrote:

The wind is blowing
the leaves are falling
the flowers are bending
the boy is lying
the water is waving
the boats are swirling
the people are being blowen
the rain is pouring
the birds are snuglen
the boots are splish splashing
the grass is wet
there is red and blue, black brown and white

It will be suggested later (see p. xxv) that children can best start writing rhythmical rhymed poetry by adapting songs.

But there are many ways in which poems can be used in prose

composition, or free writing, lessons. Some poems which suggest rather than state, which begin a story rather than finish it, are classed under MYSTERY, and may be helpful as a beginning for imaginative writing. So may those under FANTASY. It is often best simply to read the poem, well, once or twice, and then to let each child push on as his own imagination and experience dictate. It is useful, sometimes essential, to let each have a copy of the poem, to refresh his memory if need be. Those who are 'stuck' can be started off by quiet individual questions from the teacher, or by the repetition of one or two particularly striking lines. A general discussion on the 'meaning' of the poem, on the lines of 'Who do you think came to the tower?', 'Why did no one answer?' and so forth (assuming the poem to be *The Listeners* (see MYSTERY)) may merely provide ready-made answers for those who are too lazy to bother to find their own. But of course the amount of help necessary must depend on the individual child.

All sorts of poems may help children engaged in writing. For instance, each child was making a folder, containing his own story of being wrecked on a desert island, and illustrated by maps and pictures. Invention had flagged, and a great many of the class were idle. Reading A. A. Milne's *Old Sailor* (see SAILORS) with its rollicking rhythm and its long list of necessary and desirable things to do when wrecked, provided fresh impetus, and off they went again, writing busily.

The poet's lively imagination can stimulate and inspire classes of widely varying ages and abilities. A class of thirteen-year-olds, some of them barely literate, listened to and much enjoyed Ted Hughes' *My Brother Bert* (see PETS) with its account of his extraordinary pet animals. They discussed it. The teacher had snipped from illustrated magazines and colour supplements many different pictures of exotic animals, and presented one to each boy; each boy then wrote on the reactions of his own relatives should he bring his animal home as a pet. Most of the work was very creditable. The boys asked to have the poem repeated more than once, both during the lesson and some days afterwards.

5. WRITING SONGS

It is a commonplace that children should not be taught that poetry *must* rhyme. Here, excellent use can be made of Arthur Waley's translations from the Chinese (see WAL.C.P.) as examples of writing which is obviously poetry and yet clearly has no need of rhyme. Often in children's writing of poems the imagined need of rhyme will distort the sense; and such absurdities arise as in an eight-year-old's ballad of a storm at sea, when after using 'deck' and 'wreck' he suddenly introduced a flock of geese, I queried this, and was told he could only think of 'peck' as the next rhyme, and only geese—so far as he knew—'did peck'. Another charming ballad, well-sustained, written by an eleven-year-old after a train journey, collapsed heavily on the last rhymed word.

> *The whistle woke me from a dream,*
> *I looked round with joy in my heart,*
> *There's the chimneys of old Aberdeen,*
> *And my uncle waits with the cart.*

'Did your uncle bring a cart to the station? Is he a farmer?'

'Oh no, miss, he's a baker, with an Austin ... but it had to rhyme.'

But it is a pity to decide, because rhyming can be awkward, to confine children to 'intensive writing' or unrhymed free verse. We may remember that Robert Frost refused to write free verse because it was too like playing tennis with the net down, and Auden's similar objection. A compromise which can lead to exciting work is to let children write to tunes, following the example of Ben Jonson, Robert Burns and Rudyard Kipling. (Children enjoy identifying the tunes used by Kipling—they will see at once, for instance, that the popular *Smuggler's Song* see SMUGGLERS) fits precisely the tune of 'Sing a song of ixpence'.)

An easy form to begin with is that of many negro spirituals, in which each verse consists of one line repeated several times, followed by a refrain. The importance of words and stresses is appreciated when the lines are tested, as they must be, by being sung. But on the other hand, such tunes allow for much latitude in the number of syllables to a line, and the Muslim child who wrote in the middle of a carol:

> *O there was a prophet who is my Lord*
> *And he believes in nothing but God,*

found the rhyme quite adequate in a song.

Such tunes as *We shall not be moved*, *We shall overcome* and *I'm so glad* (see FREEDOM SONGS) can be used with great success. Recent experiences, when students on teaching practice have encouraged both primary and secondary children to write songs, have been most encouraging. In one Christmas play, the various groups of characters, angels, kings and shepherds, were each given a simple tune. The shepherds chose *Down by the Riverside* (see SPIRITUALS) because of the line in the original, 'I'm going to walk with the Prince of Peace'. They wrote other simple lines, and sang them as they marched to Bethlehem.

Children of every age from 7 to 13 have enjoyed the song of a poor immigrant to Pennsylvania (see U.S.A.: FARMING).

> *When I first came to this land,*
> *I was not a wealthy man.*
> *So I got myself a shack,*
> *I did what I could.*
> *And I called my shack,*
> *'Break my back'.*

His cow is called 'No milk now', his wife 'Trouble and strife', and so on through his possessions. The tune is a variation of 'Baa, baa black sheep'. Teaching eight-year-olds, I handed round an adaptation—'When I first came to this school'—with some words left blank:

> *So I got myself a . . . .*
> *I did what I could.*
> *And I called my . . . . .*
>
> *. . . . .*

One small boy immediately called out with joy 'You've made it fit us!' The children acquired 'a class' which in a window-walled school was 'Made of glass'; 'a friend' called 'Round the bend' or 'You're the end'; a pen called 'Write again'; a book that was 'Learn and Look' (an actual title); ink that was 'Blue, I think' and—a line confided rather doubtfully, in a whisper—'What a stink!' None of this is 'poetry', and yet the lines reproduce the spirit of the original with gusto, and were sung with meaning.

Twelve-year-old boys learned *The Streets of Laredo* (see COWBOYS), sang the first three verses, and completed the story by explaining the cowboy's death in some well-sustained ballads, obviously influenced by Westerns. One began:

> *A man from the mountains approached me one morning,*
> *He told me he knew of a way to live gay;*
> *He spun me a story of gold in the mountains,*
> *Before I knew it he whisked me away.*

Another cowboy was deceived by a woman:

> *She said she would help me to make me a fortune,*
> *She said she would help me line my pockets with gold,*
> *She said she would help me to find out the treasure—*
> *But I found out too late that her heart it was cold.*

Sea shanties (see SEA SHANTIES) of all songs, perhaps, have the most strongly marked rhythms, which children of all ages quickly pick up. Thirteen-year-olds, in a low stream, who were introduced to a variety of shanties, produced their own songs on

various watery themes, including the University Boat Race,
then about to take place.   The transcription is exact:

> *Oxford's going down the strait*
> *Cambridge pull but their too late*
> *I knew who'd win cos Oxford's great*
> *Oxford wins again Hooray* . . . .

> *Throw the captain in the river*
> *If its cold then he will shiver*
> *If its warm then he will say*
> *Oxford wins again Hooray*

A sense of pattern was induced by the strong rhythm and continual repetition in the shanties, and appears in another set of
verses of which the inspiration is obvious:

> *Pull the rope up, bullies, pull the rope up.*
> *Way-aye pull the rope up.*
> *I have a love in fair London town*
> *Pull the rope up cause I ain't gonna drown.*

> *Let the rope down bullies let the rope down.*
> *Way-aye let the rope down.*
> *I met my love in fair London town*
> *She got married so let the rope down.*

If the teacher makes copies of the more successful songs
(including the work of as many children as possible) and lets the
class sing them, the writers are immensely gratified—particularly
those whose prose works have never been particularly satis-
factory. And strenuous rehearsals, to get the performance
absolutely right, have been welcomed and even demanded,
when the teacher promised to 'tape' the final result.

Teachers naturally find it hard to choose poems for mixed classes
containing immigrant children who can hardly speak, let alone
read or write, English. Here the simple repeated refrains of sea

shanties are most useful—almost everyone can learn to join in 'Way, aye, blow the man down' or 'Early in the morning'. In one class West Indian children who could not write proved to be very quick at inventing rhythmic lines—these the teacher wrote on the board, and the whole class sang them. Another mixed class of top juniors wrote their own version of *Paddy works on the Railway* (see U.S.A.: RAILROADS), adapting it to the new motorways.

> O in nineteen hundred and sixty one
> We used machines which weighed a ton
>   To work upon the highway, the highway,
>   I'm bored of the highway,
> Poor Martin works on the highway.

In 1962, 'My father taught me what to do'; in 1965, 'My father taught me how to drive'. They even appreciated the linked verses in 'Hush, little baby, don't say a word' (see LULLABIES) and achieved long strings of their own.

Reference should be made to Sybil Marshall's experience, when her children wrote songs to a tune in Beethoven's Pastoral Symphony (see *An Experiment in Education* C.U.P. 1963, pp. 206–211).

6. FOR PAINTING LESSONS

It may be a pleasant and useful exercise for children to illustrate the poems they enjoy (as long as we are clear that this part of the lesson is not a *poetry* lesson). Indeed a good way to encourage children to enjoy poetry is to let each child make an individual anthology, writing out *only* the poems, or lines, he genuinely prefers, and (if he likes) enriching the pages with illustrations or decorative borders. (See once more, Sybil Marshall, op. cit. plates 28–31 for beautiful examples of this kind of children's work.)

In art lessons, reading short vivid poems, or even a few lines, can release and inspire creative activity. In this index, under PAINTING, a few poems are listed which have been used successfully for this purpose. This again must be a very personal and individual way of teaching: each teacher must choose from his own favourite poems those lines or verses which create striking visual images.

Often a verse or two from the Authorised Version of the Bible, with its powerful evocative imagery, can be read. Not only Edward Hicks' famous *Peaceable Kingdom* (see the cover of PENG.AN) but also an amazing painting by an eleven-year-old (see Sybil Marshall, op. cit. plate 2) was inspired by the words: 'The wolf shall dwell with the lamb, and the leopard shall lie down with the kid; and the calf and the young lion and the fatling together; and a little child shall lead them'.

Robert Frost's brief lyric *Stopping by Woods on a Snowy Evening* (see SNOW)—a poem appreciated by quite young children, yet containing matter enough for the most sophisticated reader—inspired some beautiful smudgy chalk drawings of the narrow track running between dark pine woods and frozen lake, in falling snow, the only definite point the tiny figure of the man with horse and sleigh, momentarily halted.

For a full and illuminating discussion of this use of poetry, see Kay Melzi, *Art in the Primary School* (Blackwell 1967).

7. FOR RELIGIOUS INSTRUCTION

The best-known carols and hymns have not been included in this index, since they are so readily available in specific collections of carols and hymns, and are so generally used. But some less well known carols, and other poems relating to Christmas and Epiphany, at many levels, have been listed. Negro spirituals, too, on a host of Old and New Testament subjects, can be found and profitably introduced.

Vachel Lindsay's *Daniel Jazz* (see DANIEL), inspired by negro rhythms, tells a familiar story in a new and (to some children) a startling way. It has been enjoyed, in my experience, by children of every age from eight upwards. Its strong, catchy, jazz rhythm and repetitive style make it one of the poems in which a class—if well led—can join without having copies of the poem in front of them. When the class can have copies, *Daniel* lends itself admirably to all sorts of different arrangements. A group can mime the action while others read the poem—either in unison, or with many different voices for the narrator, Darius, Daniel, his mother, his tender sweetheart and the rest. The more confident can read individual parts, the less confident be grouped to speak in unison as courtiers commenting, and even the least confident are always happy to growl as lions. It is very important to insist that this is a serious, though not solemn, way of telling the story, neither flippant nor irreligious.

John Heath-Stubbs and Edwin Muir have written excellent and very different ballads on Noah's Flood (see NOAH), and the former recites his own poem to great effect on the record available with *Here Today* (see HERE). Older children are interested in the unexpected point of view from which the speaker of Eliot's *Journey of the Magi* (see EPIPHANY) sees the birth of Christ, or in Betjeman's questioning about the essential meaning of '*Christmas*' (see CHRISTMAS (RELIGIOUS)).

Suggestions will be found under RELIGIOUS THEMES for other poems which teachers may care to use in this connection.

8. FOR HISTORY AND GEOGRAPHY

Literature has been described as the name given to the more readable of historical documents; certainly poems can play a part in the teaching of history, and even in some geography lessons.

History lessons can be begun, illustrated or rounded off with relevant poems and songs, often contemporary (see, for instance, ARMADA, AGINCOURT, TRAFALGAR). Talking of Charles I, we must find Marvell's noble lines on his execution highly relevant, especially as Marvell was of the other party. And there is something haunting about the anonymous snatch,

'As I was going by Charing Cross' (see CHARLES I). Various poems which might be useful have been indexed under the name of the country concerned, others appear under the names of individuals, for instance NELSON and NAPOLEON, and yet others under WAR, WARS, HUMAN RIGHTS, PROTESTS (POLITICAL) and TRADE UNIONS.

The use of poems in history lessons need not be confined to secondary work. The history of the United States, for instance, is particularly well illustrated by songs, many of which are listed in the index by subject, and many of which are quite suitable for juniors. Geographers too must be concerned with songs about pioneers, cowboys and railroads, as well as with such poems as Lindsay's *The Flower-fed Buffaloes* (see BUFFALOES), Benét's *The Ballad of William Sycamore* (see U.S.A.: PIONEERS & THE WEST) and Woody Guthrie's *So Long* (see U.S.A.: DUST BOWLS).

An actual revision lesson with a class of eight- and nine-year-olds may serve as an example. They had done a project on the settlement of the United States. Questions elicited that the early traders, finding it hard to travel through the forests, went by river in canoes and flat-boats. The four rows of double desks became flat-boats, a solitary boy in a single desk at the back was a scout in a canoe, and all paddled vigorously—and confusedly. When asked how this could be remedied, one child suggested that they could count, another that they could sing. They learned *Shenandoah* (see SEA SHANTIES) in its original version, and paddled rhythmically, singing. They appreciated that alternate lines were sung by different groups to prevent the paddlers becoming breathless, and that the song would help to keep weary arms going. Similarly, questions on the prairies led naturally to singing *Home on the Range* (see COWBOYS); consideration of the loneliness of early settlers and their lack of ready-made amusements, led to talk of play-parties and to the singing of *Skip to my Lou* (see DANCING). The children found it possible to add extra verses of their own invention—'Galloping horses, two by two' went particularly well when they sang it.

This lesson was later followed up by consideration of work-songs and their rhythms; further reinforcement of the children's work in American History was given when *Pick a Bale of Cotton* (see WORK SONGS) and *Michael, Row the Boat Ashore* (see ROWING) were sung.

Possibilities of this kind are limitless—particularly for older children, who can gain vivid pictures of the atmosphere of the Industrial Revolution from such songs as *Fourpence a Day* (see INDUSTRY) and from ballads and broadsides in such collections as *The Common Muse* (see C. MUSE). (See also FACTORIES, MACHINES, MINERS).

Attention may here be drawn to the interesting series of TOPIC and FOLKWAYS records, which contain a great number of real folksongs of many kinds. Booklets of words accompany the records, and often some historical information too. There is a useful discography of ballads and broadsides in C. MUSE.

9. ETCETERA

Some teachers have the pleasant habit of reading poems—purely for enjoyment—when there is an odd five minutes to be filled. It is sometimes possible to follow up in this way some incident which has attracted the children's attention. An accident seen on the way to school, for instance, or a road safety campaign, may appropriately lead to the introduction of Karl Shapiro's *Auto Wreck* or Ogden Nash's warning *Tweedledee and Tweedle-doom* (see ACCIDENTS). The latter is an excellent example, too, of how to convey a serious message without being solemn or pompous.

Even a minor disturbance in the classroom can be used to advantage. A large bee, buzzing continuously round the room and against the window, had to be caught and removed. The lesson (to eight-year-olds) recovered from the interruption and finished a few minutes early. 'Do you remember the noise the bee made?' asked the teacher. Then, to a chorus of subdued buzzing, she read de la Mare's *Bees' Song* (see BEES) and fascinated at least one child, who recounted the incident.

After a country walk through blossoming beanfields, another class was delighted to find that John Clare had revelled in the same experience (see BEANFIELDS).

It may have been noticed that I have laid great emphasis upon *enjoyment* of poetry. At least I am in good company. Sir Philip Sidney wrote that the end of poesie is 'to teach and delight'; Dr. Johnson declared that 'the end of poetry is to instruct by pleasing'; Robert Frost said that a poem 'begins in delight and ends in wisdom'. I hope that this book may help teachers to find poems which will both delight and enlighten their classes.

Cambridge 1966   HELEN MORRIS

The Grouping of Poems

The poems are grouped under their subjects, but certain *kinds* of poems will be found under the following headings: CLERI-HEWS, COUNTING RHYMES, COUNTING-OUT RHYMES, FABLES, LIMERICKS, NONSENSE, QUESTION & ANSWER, RIDDLES, TALES (CAUTIONARY) and TALES (TALL).

The poems are arranged alphabetically, by title, under each heading. The articles, 'A', 'An' and 'The' have been ignored. When only part of a poem is cited, the title is followed by the word (Part).

Explanation of the letters and numbers following each poem will be found on p. 273.

The Index

ACTORS
The Forbidden Play, ROBERT GRAVES
  I'll tell you the truth, father, though your heart bleed
    GRA.FID 40

AEROPLANES
Flight to Australia, C. DAY LEWIS
  Sing we the two lieutenants, Parer and M'Intosh
    PEG V 6   TW.N 40

Flight to Australia (Part), C. DAY LEWIS
  And now the earth they had spurned
  rose up against them in anger
    FAB.M.V 272

Landscape near an Aerodrome, STEPHEN SPENDER
  More beautiful and soft than any moth
    ECHO III 92   P.F.P II I 57

On the Wings of the Morning, J. DAY
  A sudden roar, a mighty rushing sound
    PEG V 3

AGE
See **Old Age**

AGINCOURT
The Ballad of Agincourt, MICHAEL DRAYTON
  Fair stood the wind for France
    AN.E.P 33   ECHO I I9   FAB.C.V 237
    IRON I 6I   P.F.P II 67   P.W 58

ALE
Back and Sides go Bare, ANON
  I cannot eat but little meat
    WHEEL III 52

Bring us in good Ale, ANON
  Bring us in good ale, and bring us in good ale
    WHEEL III 50

ALEXANDER THE GREAT
Alexander the Great, ANON
>Four men stood by the grave of a man
>>COME 191   P.W 30

ALPHABET RHYMES
See also OX.N.R 105–9

A was once an apple-pie, EDWARD LEAR
>A was once an apple-pie
>>FAB.N.V 186

Alphabet, ANON
>A B C D E F G
>>BL.J I 21

An Apple-Pie, ANON
>A was an apple-pie
>>PUF.N.R 12
>A Apple-pye! B bit it
>>TOM.T.G 25

Tom Thumb's Alphabet, ANON
>A was an archer who shot at a frog
>>MER 232
>A was an archer
>>FAB.N.V 43

AMERICA
See also **United States**

There was an Indian, J. C. SQUIRE
>There was an Indian
>>COME 379   P.F.P I 181   P.LIFE IV 50
>>SCH.M.V 158

ANGER
A Poison Tree, WILLIAM BLAKE
>I was angry with my friend
>>BLA.P 54   M.R.CHA 57   P.REM 177
>>P.W 141   WHEEL I 62

ANIMALS

See throughout A.A., B.B.F, F.FEET, PEL.AN, PENG.AN

See also **Animals, Fantastic: Birds: Fishes and Sea Creatures: Insects: Noah: Pets: Reptiles: Spiders: Zoo**

See also **Apes and Monkeys: Badgers: Bats: Bears: Buffaloes: Bullfrogs: Bulls: Camels: Cats: Cattle: Cheetahs: Cows,** See **Cattle: Coyotes: Deer: Dogs,** See also **Puppies: Donkeys: Elephants: Foxes: Frogs: Giraffes: Gnus: Hares: Hedgehogs: Hippopotami: Horses: Jaguars: Kangaroos: Lambs: Lions: Llamas: Mice: Moles: Monkeys,** See **Apes: Mules: Otters, Oxen: Pigs: Ponies,** See **Horses: Puppies: Rabbits: Rats: Seals: Sheep: Sloths: Squirrels: Stags: Tigers: Toads: Tortoises: Whales: Wolves: Yaks**

Allie, call the Birds in, ROBERT GRAVES

    Allie, call the birds in

B.P II 30	DAWN 46	GRA.FID I I
GRA.PENG 24	MER 252	OX.V.J I 50
PAT 64	TREE IV 26	

The Animals, WALT WHITMAN

    I think I could turn and live with the animals,
        they are so placid and self-contained

A.A I30	B.B.F I4	M.R.CHA 89
MY I29	PEG III 45	PENG.AN I 5
P.SING 45	P.W 20I	

Animals' Houses, JAMES REEVES

    Of animals' houses

PUF.Q 75	REE.W.M 25

The Bells of Heaven, RALPH HODGSON

    'Twould ring the bells of heaven

A.A I29	AN.METH I09	AN.SPO I I23
M.R.FEEL 39	P.F.P I 95	P.P.TALK 7I
TOM.T.G 82		

ANIMALS, FANTASTIC
See throughout BEL.PUF, REE.P.A; also FAB.N.V 75, 77, 82, 166
See also **Tales, Tall**

The Common Cormorant, ANON
 The common cormorant, or shag
   A.D.L 227   G.TR.P 223   PENG.COM 240
   P.P.WIDE 41   P.TONG 123

The Crocodile, ANON
 Now listen you landsmen unto me
   KEY I 45   PENG.M.C 258   P.P.WIDE 14
   P.TONG 95   P.W 24

The Derby Ram, ANON
 As I went down to Derby Town
   B.B.F 195   BL.J IV 23   ECHO II 8
   FAB.N.V 70   KEY III 126   MER 173
   OX.N.R 205   PEG I 46   PENG.A.F.S 32 (G,P)
   S.T.S. I 18 (G)

The Doze, JAMES REEVES
 Through dangly woods the aimless Doze
   M.R. FEEL 18   REE.P.A 13

The Hippocrump, JAMES REEVES
 Along the valley of the Ump
   HAP 45   REE.P.A 5   TREE III 92

The Lady and the Bear, THEODORE ROETHKE
 A Lady came to a Bear by a Stream
   V.F 129

The Serpent, THEODORE ROETHKE
 There was a Serpent who had to sing
   V.F 128

The Tale of Custard the Dragon, OGDEN NASH
 Belinda lived in a little white house
   G.TR.P 166   NA.P.B 80   WEALTH 204

AUSTRALIA
See also **Transportation**

The Banks of the Condamine, ANON
>   Oh, hark the dogs are barking, love
>   FAB.BAL 231

In the Droving Days, A. B. PATERSON
>   'Only a pound', said the auctioneer
>   SPIR 52

The New-Chum's First Trip, ANON
>   Now if you will listen I'll tell you a story
>   FAB.BAL 232

Waltzing Matilda, A. B. PATERSON
>   Once a jolly swagman camped by a billabong
>   CHER 138   FIRE.F.S 216 (P)   KEY I 98
>   MER 344

The Wild Colonial Boy, ANON
>   'Tis of a wild colonial boy, Jack Doolan was his name
>   FAB.BAL 229

AUTUMN
See also **Harvest: Months**

Autumn, T. E. HULME
>   A touch of cold in the autumn night
>   FLA 40   MY 10   P.W 252

Autumn, JOHN CLARE
>   I love the fitful gust that shakes
>   AN.SPO II 72   KEY I 74   M.R.FEEL 51
>   PEG II 7   P.SING 20

Autumn, EMILY DICKINSON
>   The morns are meeker than they were
>   JOY 43

Autumn, JOHN CLARE
>   The thistledown's flying, though the winds are all still
>   KEY III 16   P.W 186

Autumn Fires, R. L. STEVENSON
    In the other gardens
        M.R.FEEL 52   OX.V.J I 46   TREE II 45

The Autumn Wind, WU-TI TRANS WALEY
    Autumn wind rises; white clouds fly
        WAL.C.P 42

The Burning of the Leaves, LAURENCE BINYON
    Now is the time for the burning of the leaves
        PENG.C.V 50   PEG IV 42

Field of Autumn, LAURIE LEE
    Slow moves the acid breath of noon
        THEME 31

Late Autumn, ANDREW YOUNG
    The boy called to his team
        KEY IV 38   YOU.P 32

November Night, A. CRAPSEY
    Listen . . .
        WEALTH 225

October's Song, ELEANOR FARJEON
    The forest's afire !
        A.D.L. 99

Ode to Autumn, JOHN KEATS
    Season of mists and mellow fruitfulness
        CH.GAR 95   COME 220   D.P.F.F 58
        ECHO II 52   G.TR.P 279   IRON II 170
        M.R.CHA 44   PAT 54   PEG III 18
        P.F.P II 30   P.P.WIDE 60   P.SING 18
        P.W 186   R.R 87   TOM.T.G 163
        WEALTH 56   WHEEL IV 112

Rich Days, W. H. DAVIES
    Welcome to you, rich autumn days
        PEG III 17

BAGPIPES

The Piper o' Dundee, ANON
> The piper came to our town
> > OX.V.J II 82   PEG II 59   P.P.TALK 33

BALACLAVA

The Charge of the Light Brigade, LORD TENNYSON
> Half a league, half a league
> > AN.SPO I 155   M.R.HAND 40   PEG II 50

BALDER: BALDER'S FUNERAL

Balder Dead (Part), ANON
> But when the gods and heroes heard, they brought
> > AN.SPO I 91

BALDNESS

On this Baldness, CHINESE TRANS WALEY
> At dawn I sighed to see my hairs fall
> > WAL.C.P 182

BALLADS, RIDDLING

Jennifer, Gentle and Rosemary, ANON
> There were three sisters fair and bright
> > AN.SPO I 73   BAL 48, 50   BUN 94
> > COME 333   FAB.BAL 25   FAB.C.V 281
> > KEY I 86   MER 310   OX.L.V 94
> > PEG II 60   WHEEL I 23

BALLET

Song of the Ballet, J. B. MORTON
> Lift her up tenderly
> > PEG II 101

BALLOONS

The Balloons, OSCAR WILDE
    Against these turbid turquoise skies
        OX.V.J IV 69   PEG V 24

BANDS

The Ceremonial Band, JAMES REEVES
    The old king of Dorchester
        M.R.FEEL 5   TREE II 78

BANJOS

The Banjo Player, C. DYMENT
    The scarlet buses splashed their way
        OX.V.J IV 50

BARLEY

John Barleycorn, ANON
    There were three kings into the East
    There came three men from out the West
        ECHO I 81   FAB.BAL I 56   KEY II 92
        OX.S.M.J II 29 (M)   PEG IV 39

The Ripe and Bearded Barley, ANON
    Come out, 'tis now September
        DRUM 86

BATHING

East Anglian Bathe, JOHN BETJEMAN
    Oh when the early morning at the seaside
        ALB I 24   A.D.L 75   BET.P 128

North-Easter, IAN SERRAILLIER
    I love the north-easter
        SER.HAP 26

BATS

Bat, D. H. LAWRENCE
> At evening, sitting on this terrace
>> MOD 118   PENG.AN 30   P.F.P I 125
>> P.TONG 9   P.W 255   UNDER 88
>> WHEEL III 155

The Bat, THEODORE ROETHKE
> By day the bat is cousin to the mouse
>> MY 125

The Bat, RUTH PITTER
> Lightless, unholy, eldritch thing
>> A.D.L 162   DAWN 67   WEALTH 72

The Bat, OGDEN NASH
> Myself, I rather like the bat
>> NA.P.B 50   NA.P.D.R 114   TREE IV 49

Man and Bat, D. H. LAWRENCE
> When I went into my room, at mid-morning
>> LAW.PENG 91

BATTLES
See **Sea Battles**
See **Agincourt: Balaclava: Blenheim: Corunna**

BEACHES
See **Bathing: Seaside**

BEANFIELDS

The Beanfield, JOHN CLARE
> A beanfield in blossom smells as sweet
>> PEG IV 51

Field Path, JOHN CLARE
> The beans in blossom with their spots of jet
>> IRON II 47

BEARS

The Bear, FREDERICK BROWN
  His sullen shaggy-rimmed eyes followed my every move
   EV.M 21

BED

See also **Rising Early: Waking**

Bed in Summer, R. L. STEVENSON
  In winter I get up at night
   P.LIFE I 67   PUF.V 137   TOM.T.G 90
   TREE I 18

Escape at Bedtime, R. L. STEVENSON
  The lights from the parlour and kitchen shone out
   A.D.L 268   G.TR.P 13   P.LIFE II 80
   P.REM 42

Matthew, Mark, Luke and John, ANON
  Matthew, Mark, Luke and John
   BL.J.I 7   B.P I 21   CH.GAR 143
   COME 466   C.S.B 84 (P)   MER 134
   OX.V.J II 17   OX.L.V 87   P.P.FACT 74
   PUF.V 269   TOM.T.G 202

BEECHES

The Beech and the Sapling Oak, T. L. PEACOCK
  For the tender beech and the sapling oak
   KEY IV 23

Beech Leaves, JAMES REEVES
  In autumn down the beechwood path
   A.D.L 99

BEES

The Bee-Boy's Song, RUDYARD KIPLING
  Bees! Bees! hark to your bees
   KIP.INC 575

Bees Song, WALTER DE LA MARE
>   Thouzandz of thornz there be
>> DE LA M.P II 244   PENG.M.C 190   P.P.OVER 26
>> V.F 51

BEETLES

Rendezvous with a Beetle, E. V. RIEU
>   Meet me in Usk
>> P.LIFE III 73   PUF.Q 114

BEGGARS

The Jovial (or Jolly) Beggar, ANON
>   There was a jovial beggar
>> DRUM 82   TREE III 80

BELLS

See also PUF.N.R 46–7 (for the youngest)

Bells, JAMES REEVES
>   Hard as crystal
>> REE.W.M 58

The Bells (Part), E. A. POE
>   Hear the sledges with the bells
>> CH.GAR 175   P.SING 141   PUF.V 29
>> TREE IV 65

The Bells of London, ANON
>   The bells of London all fell wrangling
>> M.R.FEEL 62

The Bells of Shandon, F. MAHONEY
>   With deep affection
>> P.P.BRA 33

Bredon Hill, A. E. HOUSMAN
>   In summertime on Bredon
>> DRUM 44

London Bells (Oranges and Lemons), ANON
Gay go up and gay go down

B.P I 74	EX.T.TRA 14	MER 60
OX.L.V 259	OX.N.R 68	P.P.SAL 61
PUF.V 178	TREE I 46	

Ring out, Wild Bells, LORD TENNYSON
Ring out, wild bells, to the wild sky
P.SING 146

Wantage Bells, JOHN BETJEMAN
Now with the bells through the apple bloom
WEALTH 228

BENBOW, ADMIRAL

The Death of Admiral Benbow, ANON
Come all you sailors bold

C.MUSE 124	ECHO II 20	IRON II 16
MER 260	OX.P.C 44	P.TONG 18

BIBLE
See **Religious Themes**

BICYCLING

Mulga Bill's Bicycle, A. B. PATERSON
Twas Mulga Bill, from Eaglehawk,
that caught the cycling craze
M.R.ON 93

BIRCHES

Birches, ROBERT FROST
When I see birches bend to left and right

FRO.P I 52	FRO.PENG 81	FRO.YOU 36
HAP 55	PENG.M.A.V 54	

BIRDCATCHERS

The Birdcatcher's Boy, THOMAS HARDY
Father I fear your trade
KEY I 69

BIRDS
See also **Blackbirds: Buzzards: Canaries: Choughs: Cocka-
toos: Cocks: Corbies,** See **Ravens: Cormorants:
Cranes: Crows: Cuckoos: Ducks: Eagles: Flycatchers:
Geese: Goldfinches: Gulls: Hawks: Hens: Humming-
birds: Jackdaws: Kookaburras: Larks: Linnets: Mal-
lard: Martins: Nightingales: Owls: Parrots: Pelicans:
Penguins: Pewits: Pigeons: Quails: Ravens: Robins:
Sea Birds: Sedgewarblers: Shags: Sparrows: Swans:
Thrushes: Tits: Vultures: Wagtails: Woodlarks:
Woodpeckers: Wrens**

Allie call the Birds in, ROBERT GRAVES
Allie, call the birds in

B.P II 30	DAWN 46	GRA.FID 11
GRA.PENG 24	MER 252	OX.V.J I 50
PAT 64	TREE IV 26	

The Bird Escaped, ANN PRESTON
Unsuspecting hopping gaily
EV.M 18

Bird Talk, AILEEN FISHER
'Think . . . ' said the robin
V.F 64

Birds, RAY FABRIZIO
A bird flies and has wings
MY 137

The Birds, CZECH CAROL
From out of a wood did a cuckoo fly, cuckoo
OX.S.M.J I 15

Birds at Winter Nightfall, THOMAS HARDY
Around the house the flakes fly faster
HAR.SEL 28

Birds' Nests, EDWARD THOMAS
The summer nests uncovered by autumn wind
THO.SEL 60

BLACKSMITHS
See also **Farriers**

Brand the Blacksmith, JAMES REEVES
  Brand the blacksmith with his hard hammer
    KEY III 108

BLENHEIM

The Battle of Blenheim, ROBERT SOUTHEY
  It was a summer evening
    G.TR.P 146   KEY III 68

BLESSINGS
See **Graces: Prayers**

BLINDNESS

The Blind Men and the Elephant, J. SAXE
  It was six men of Indostan
    A.A 115   G.TR.P 200   KEY III 40
    OX.V.J II 63
The Fog, W. H. DAVIES
  I saw the fog grow thick
    BL.J III 5   KEY IV 128   PEG I 103
Test Match at Lords, ALAN ROSS
  Bailey bowling, McLean cuts him late for one
    KEY IV 130
With Half an Eye, PHILIP HOBSBAUM
  At seven the sun that lit my world blew out
    HAP 92

BLITZ

The Streets of Laredo, LOUIS MACNIECE
  O early one morning I walked out like Agag
    (for original model, see **Cowboys**)
    CHER 309   FLA 111   RIS 112

BLONDIN

Blondin, WALTER DE LA MARE
 With clinging dainty catlike tread
  R.R 27

BOARS

Old Bangum, ANON
 There is a wild boar in these woods
  BAL 103

BOATS

Alone in a Boat, A SCHOOLCHILD
 Speeding along like a gull on the wind
  WHEEL I 171

Sampan, CHINESE POEM
 Waves lap lap
  WEALTH 3

BOATS, PAPER

Paper Boats (Part), RABINDRANATH TAGORE
 Day by day I float my paper boats
  one by one down the running stream
  A.D.L 159

BONFIRES
See also **Guy Fawkes' Night**

Autumn Fires, R. L. STEVENSON
 In the other gardens
  M.R.FEEL 52   OX.V.J I 46   TREE II 45

The Burning of the Leaves, LAURENCE BINYON
 Now is the time for the burning of the leaves
  PENG.C.V 50   PEG IV 42

BOOKS

A Book, EMILY DICKINSON
>   He ate and drank the precious words
>   JOY 155

O for a Booke, ANON
>   O for a booke and a shadie nooke
>   COME 147   DRUM 64

A Second-Hand Bookshop, JOHN ARLOTT
>   The sunlight filters through the panes
>   ALB I 3

BOOTH, GENERAL WILLIAM

General William Booth enters into Heaven, VACHEL LINDSAY
>   Booth led boldly with his big bass drum
>   FAB.M.V 158   LIN.P 123   SPIR 97

BOSTON

Boston, ANON
>   I come from the city of Boston
>   PEG II 75

BOXING

First Fight, VERNON SCANNELL
>   Tonight, then, is the night
>   MY 72

BOYS

See also **Brothers: Tales, Cautionary (Belloc): Teenagers**

Aubade: Dick the Donkey-boy, OSBERT SITWELL
>   Tall, with tow-hair, the texture of hide
>   DAWN 76

The Boy who laughed at Santa Claus, OGDEN NASH
>   In Baltimore there lived a boy
>   KEY III 85

Lamb, HUMBERT WOLFE
    The old bellwether
        OX.V.J III 31

The Naughty Boy, JOHN KEATS
    There was a naughty boy

A.D.L 200	B.P I 19	FAB.C.V 284
FAB.N.V 99	MER 204	MY 107
OX.V.J I 32	P.P.OVER 14	PUF.V 122
TREE II 36		

Portrait of a Boy, S. V. BENÉT
    After the whipping he crawled into bed
        PEG III 87

The Rescue, HAL SUMMERS
    The boy climbed up into the tree
        DAWN 58

Timothy Winters, CHARLES CAUSLEY
    Timothy Winters comes to school

COM 170	HERE 15	MY 100
UNDER 59	WHEEL II 167	

Tired Tim, WALTER DE LA MARE
    Poor tired Tim! It's sad for him
        DE LA M.P. II 112   EX.T.H 38   F.Y.D 67

BRICKLAYERS

A Truthful Song I, RUDYARD KIPLING
    I tell this tale which is strictly true
        KIP.INC 635   P.P.OVER 86

BROTHERS

My Brother Bert, TED HUGHES
    Pets are the hobby of my brother Bert
        HU.MEET 25   WHEEL I 165

The Twins, HENRY S. LEIGH
   In form and feature, face and limb

D.P.JOU 30	EX.T.CH 92	G.TR.P 232
KEY II 114		

BUCCANEERS
See **Pirates**

BUFFALOES

The Buffalo, HERBERT PRICE
   Encased in mud, and breathing valley steam
   P. SING 192

The Flower-fed Buffaloes, VACHEL LINDSAY
   The flower-fed buffaloes of the spring

CHER 124	PEG V 19	PENG.M.A.V 70
P.F.P II 232	THIS.W.D 123	

BUGLES

No one cares less than I, EDWARD THOMAS
   No one cares less than I
   THO.GR 84

Song, LORD TENNYSON
   The splendour falls on castle walls

A.D.L 216	AN.E.P 137	AN.SPO.II 142
CH.GAR 28	COME 122	D.P.ROAD 95
OX.V.J II 88	P.P.FAL 55	P.SING 148
P.W 191	THIS.W.D 86	TOM.T.G 196
WEALTH 216		

BULLFROGS

Bullfrog, TED HUGHES
   With their lithe long strong legs
   DAWN 65

BUZZARDS

The Buzzards, MARTIN ARMSTRONG
> When evening came and the warm glow grew deeper
> P.SING 42

CALAIS

The Winning of Cales (c. 1596), THOMAS DELONEY
> Long the proud Spaniard
> C.MUSE 74   D.P.ROAD 102   P.TONG 80
> WHEEL I 39

CAMELS

Commissariat Camels, RUDYARD KIPLING
> We haven't a camelty tune of our own
> KIP.INC 559

Exile, V. SHEARD
> Ben-Arabie was the camel
> ALB I 157

The Plaint of the Camel, C. E. CARYL
> Canary-birds feed on sugar and seed
> KEY I 25   M.R.ON 58

CANALS

The Erie Canal, ANON
> We were forty miles from Albany forget it I never shall
> B.L.A.F.S 146 (G,P)   IVES 228 (G,P)
> PENG.A.F.S 46 (G,P)   S.N.W 44 (G,P)

CANARIES

The Canary, OGDEN NASH
> The song of canaries
> NA.P.B 79   PENG.M.C 170

CAPITAL PUNISHMENT
See **Hanging**

CARTERS

The Carter and his Team, ANON
I was once a bold fellow and went with a team
M.R.HAND 62   TREE III 21

CATERPILLARS

The Caterpillar, CHRISTINA ROSSETTI
Brown and furry
F.FEET I 30   F.Y.D 49   G.TR.P 73
KEY I 112   MER 92

The Caterpillar, OGDEN NASH
I find among the poems of Schiller
KEY I 112   NA.P.D.R 36

The Tickling Rhyme, IAN SERRAILLIER
'Who's that tickling my back?' said the wall
KEY I 113   P.LIFE III 87

CATS
See also **Curses**
See PUF.N.R 20–1 and 140–1 (for the youngest)

The Bird Escaped, ANN PRESTON
Unsuspecting hopping gaily
EV.M 18

Cat! ELEANOR FARJEON
Cat!/Scat!
HAP 65   M.R.ON 54   OX.P.C 104
P.LIFE III 82   PUF.Q 38   TREE III 90

The Cat, RICHARD CHURCH
Hark! She is calling to her cat
M.R.HAND 58

A Cat, EDWARD THOMAS
  She had a name among the children
      R.R 183   THO.GR 41   THO.SEL 43

The Cat, W. H. DAVIES
  Within that porch, across the way
      KEY II 86   MER 257

The Cat and the Bird, G. CANNING
  Tell me, tell me, gentle Robin
      CHER 118

The Cat and the Moon, W. B. YEATS
  The cat went here and there
      A.D.L 178   OX.V.J IV 80   THIS.W.D 23
      WEALTH 2

Cats, A. S. J. TESSIMOND
  Cats, no less liquid than their shadows
      A.D.L 179   ALB I 166   KEY IV 162
      PEG IV 14   P.TIME 215

Cats, ELEANOR FARJEON
  Cats sleep
      BL.J I 13   TREE I 32

The Cats, JAN STRUTHER
  In Sycamore Square
      PEG I 36

Choosing their Names, THOMAS HOOD
  Our old cat has kittens three
      TREE III 56

Diamond cut Diamond, E. MILNE
  Two cats
      FAB.C.V 76   KEY IV 62   PENG.COM 279
      P.REM 191

Double Dutch, WALTER DE LA MARE
  That crafty cat, a buff-black Siamese
      HAP 50

Esther's Tom Cat, TED HUGHES
    Daylong this tomcat lies stretched flat
        PENG.AN 59   PENG.NEW I 52

Five Eyes, WALTER DE LA MARE
   In Hans' old mill his three black cats
            A.A 3   DE LA M.CH 30   DE LA M.P II 206
            D.P.JOU I3   EX.T.CH I I   FAB.N.V 28
            KEY I 40   MER I08   M.R.FEEL 37
            OX.V.J IV 39

Kilkenny Cats, ANON
    There once were two cats of Kilkenny
        KEY I I IO

The Kitten and the Falling Leaves, WILLIAM WORDSWORTH
   See the kitten on the wall
            B.B.F 64   G.TR.P 52   OX.P.C I06
            PAT I98   PUF.V 48   TREE IV 48

The Lost Cat, E. V. RIEU
   She took a last and simple meal
      when there were none to see her steal—
        PUF.Q I02

Milk for the Cat, HAROLD MUNRO
   When tea is brought at five o'clock
            A.A 5   AN.METH I6I   AN.SPO I I34
            D.P.ROAD I4   F.Y.D 76   G.TR.P 47
            MOD 92   MY I30   OX.P.C I09
            P.F.P I 40   P.P.TALK 43   SCH.M.V I I7
            THIS.W.D 2I

Miss Tibbles, IAN SERRAILLIER
   Miss Tibbles is my kitten; white
        PUF.Q I55

Moon, WILLIAM JAY SMITH
   I have a white cat whose name is Moon
        V.F I 54

C

Skimbleshanks: The Railway Cat, T. S. ELIOT
>   There's a whisper down the line at 11.49

CH.GAR 52	D.P.WAY 30	EX.T.CH 156
FAB.C.V 285	M.R.ON 51	PENG.M.C 164
P.P.OVER 74	V.F 58	WHEEL I 149

Song of the Jellicles, T. S. ELIOT
>   Jellicle Cats come out tonight

EX.T.TRO 10	FAB.C.V 75	FAB.N.V 175
OX.P.C 105	P.P. FACT 10	

CATTLE
See also **Bulls: Oxen**

Cattle in Trucks, E. L. M. KING
>   Poor cows, poor·sheep
>   TREE II 35

Cattle in Winter, JONATHAN SWIFT
>   The Scottish hinds, too poor to house
>   KEY II 40

Country Idyll, FRANCES CORNFORD
>   Deep in the stable tied with rope
>   KEY III 145

The Cow, R. L. STEVENSON
>   The friendly cow all red and white

F.FEET 30	MY 124	OX.P.C 116
P.LIFE I 46	PUF.V 46	

The Cow, THEODORE ROETHKE
>   There Once was a Cow with a Double Udder
>   TREE IV 60

The Cow in Apple Time, ROBERT FROST
>   Something inspires the only cow of late
>   FRO.YOU 53   PENG.M.A.V 56

Cows, JAMES REEVES
>   Half the time they munched the grass
>   and all the time they lay

OX.P.C 118	PUF.Q 64	TREE IV 50

CAVALIERS

Marching Along, ROBERT BROWNING
    Kentish Sir Byng stood for his king
        M.R.HAND 34

CAVALRY

The Charge of the Light Brigade, LORD TENNYSON
    Half a league, half a league
        AN.SPO I 155   M.R.HAND 40   PEG II 50

CELERY

Celery, OGDEN NASH
    Celery, raw
        NA.P.B I 59   V.F 104   WEALTH 24

CENTIPEDES

The Centipede, MRS. E. CRASTER
    A centipede was happy quite
        KEY I 55   PENG.YET 83

CHARCOAL BURNERS

The Penny Whistle, EDWARD THOMAS
    The new moon hangs like an ivory bugle
        OX.V.J IV 40   THO.GR 62

The Pigs and the Charcoal Burner, WALTER DE LA MARE
    The Old Pig said to the little pigs
        DE LA M.P II 205   F.FEET 86   IRON I 106
        OX.V.J II 37

CHARDIN

Still Life, WALTER DE LA MARE
    Bottle, coarse tumbler, loaf of bread
        AN.JEN 75   DE LA M.CH 72

CHARLES I

As I was going by Charing Cross, ANON
>   As I was going by Charing Cross
>>
>> COME 188　　　　FAB.C.V 109　　　FAB.N.V 261
>> OX.N.R 81　　　　OX.P.C 146　　　P.TONG 7
>> PUF.N.R 53　　　　TOM.T.G 181

Hide and Seek, HUGH CHESTERMAN
>   King Charles the First to Parliament came
>> M.R.HAND 37

An Horatian Ode (Part), ANDREW MARVELL
>   He nothing common did or mean
>> A.B.L.P 224　　　　CHER 378　　　ECHO II 25

CHARLES II

On Charles II, EARL OF ROCHESTER
>   Here lies our Sovereign Lord and King
>> G.TR.P 237　　　　PEG I 3　　　P.P.BRA 75
>> R.R 97

CHARMS & SPELLS
See also **Magic: Magicians: Witches**
See OX.N.R 74–5

Apples, ANON
>   Here's to thee
>> OX.V.J I 21

As we dance round, ANON
>   As we dance round a-ring a-ring
>> EX.T.H 43

Bethsabe's Song, GEORGE PEELE
>   Hot sun, cool fire, tempered with sweet air
>> OX.L.V 110

The Blind-worm, WILFRID GIBSON
>   When I stroked his cold dry skin
>> ALB II 63

A Charm, ROBERT HERRICK
    If ye fear to be affrighted
        CHER 167

A Charm, RUDYARD KIPLING
    Take of English earth as much
        JOY 3   KIP.INC 492

A Charm against the Toothache, JOHN HEATH-STUBBS
    Venerable Mother Toothache
        DAWN 53   MY 159   FENG.C.V 307

Come, butter, come, ANON
    Come, butter, come
        OX.V.J 1 19

Cush-a-Cow bonny, ANON
    Cush-a-cow bonny, come let down your milk
        OX.V.J 1 19

Gently dip, GEORGE PEELE
    Gently dip, but not too deepe
        CHER 174   PENG.E.V 26   THIS.W.D 66

Good Wish, ANON
    Power of raven be thine
        FAB.C.V 229

Goose and Gander, ANON
    Grey goose and gander
        B.B.F 195   CHER 174   MER 113

Here we come a-piping, ANON
    Here we come a-piping
        EX.T.H 43

Hist Whist, E. E. CUMMINGS
    Hist Whist
        MER 113

Luriana, Lurilee, CHARLES ELTON
    Come out and climb the garden path
        P.P.BRA 67

CHIMNEYSWEEPS

CHOUGHS

Chough, R. E. WARNER
    Desolate that cry as though world were unworthy
        ECHO II 21

CHRIST

The Birds, H. BELLOC
    When Jesus Christ was four years old
        BEL.S.V III   F.Y.D 61

In the Wilderness, ROBERT GRAVES
    Christ of his gentleness

B.B.F 212	COME 109	EV.M 105
GRA.FID 33	GRA.PENG 13	R.R 166

My dancing day, ANON
    Tomorrow shall be my dancing day
        C.S.B 78 (P)   MER 296

Yet if his Majesty our Sovereign Lord, ANON
    Yet if his Majesty our Sovereign Lord

AN.SPO II 59	COME 484	D.P.F.F 182
FAB.C.V 364	PEG V 102	P.P.WIDE 95
R.R 156	WEALTH 285	WHEEL I 44

CHRISTMAS (RELIGIOUS)
See also **Epiphany**
See also CHER 411–26

Bethlehem, ROBERT SOUTHWELL
    Behold a silly tender babe

G.TR.P 287	OX.V.J III 83	THIS.W.D 94

The Birds, CZECH CAROL
    From out of a wood did a cuckoo fly, cuckoo
        OX.S.M.J I 15 (M)

CHRISTMAS (SECULAR)

See also CHER 411–26

Christmas, LOUIS MACNEICE
>A week to Christmas, cards of snow and holly
>>WHEEL III 179

The Twelve Days of Christmas, ANON
>On the first day of Christmas

>>| | | |
>>|---|---|---|
>>| B.P II 11 | EX.T.H 53 | FIRE F.S 248 (P) |
>>| F.S.N.A 245 (G,B) | KEY III 47 | MER 238 |
>>| M.R.ON 104 | OX.L.V 206 | OX.N.R 198 |
>>| OX.S.M.S I 14 (M) | P.LIFE III 56 | P.P.FACT 40 |
>>| PUF.N.R 184 | | |

A Visit from Saint Nicholas, CLEMENT MOORE
>'Twas the night before Christmas, when all through the
>house
>>P.LIFE I 73

The Yule Days, ANON
>The king sent his lady on the first Yule day
>>CHER 415

CHRISTMAS TREES

The Christmas Tree, C. DAY LEWIS
>Put out the lights now!
>>SCH.M.V 69 WHEEL II 149

Little Tree, E. E. CUMMINGS
>Little tree
>>CUM.PENG 10

CHRYSANTHEMUMS

The Last Chrysanthemum, THOMAS HARDY
>Why should this flower delay so long
>>HAR.SEL 2 THEME 58

CHURCH GOING

In Church, WILLIAM BARNES
>The Church do seem a touching sight
>>WEALTH 291

CIRCUSES
See also **Acrobats: Tightropes: Trapezes**

Circus, M. G. CHUTE
>Giraffes are tall
>>BL.J I 17

Circus Lion, C. DAY LEWIS
>Lumbering haunches, pussyfoot tread, a pride of
>>UNDER 42

Two Performing Elephants, D. H. LAWRENCE.
>He stands with his forefeet on the drum
>>PEG IV 17

CITIES & TOWNS
See also **Boston: Hiroshima: London: Rome: Teignmouth**

Beleaguered Cities, F. L. LUCAS
>Build your houses, build your houses, build your towns
>>ALB I 100

Ice Cart, WILFRID GIBSON
>Perched on my city office-stool

AN.METH 87	AN.SPO I 115	D.P.F.F 77
M.R.CHA 112	PEG II 2	P.F.P II 41
P.SING 73	SCH.M.V 59	WHEEL II 139

In the Cities, D. H. LAWRENCE
>In the cities
>>WEALTH 271

Morning at the Window, T. S. ELIOT
>They are rattling breakfast plates in basement kitchens
>>AN.E.P 178   PEG III 63   WEALTH 273

The Planster's Vision, JOHN BETJEMAN
>> Cut down that timber! Bells too many and strong
>>> BET.P 120   PENG.C.V 177   R.R 69
>>> THEME 146

The Plum Tree, B. BRECHT TRANS E. MORGAN
>> The backyard has a tiny plum-tree
>>> EV.M 41

Preludes, T. S. ELIOT
>> The winter evening settles down
>>> COM 73   DAWN 105   D.P.F.F 66
>>> EL.P 21   FLA 61   MOD 141
>>> P.W 259   WEALTH 274

To See the Rabbit, ALAN BROWNJOHN
>> We are going to see the rabbit
>>> HAP 36   JA.PO 15   PENG.AN 261

CLERIHEWS (E. C. BENTLEY)

J. S. Mill, Lord Clive, George III, Savonarola
>> OX.L.V 508–9

Dr. W. G. Grace
>> PEG IV 3   V.F 22

Empress Poppea, Cecil B. de Mille, Diodorus Siculus, Emperor Arcadius, Jonathan Swift, Geoffrey Chaucer, Abraham Lincoln
>> PENG.M.C 287–8

Sir Christopher Wren, Professor James Dewar, F.R.S.
>> P.P.FAL 36–7

George Hirst, Lord Clive
>> P.P.OVER 27

CLIMBING
See **Mountaineering**

CLOUDS

White Sheep, W. H. DAVIES
　　White sheep, white sheep
　　　　BL.J I 51

COCKATOOS

The Red Cockatoo, PO CHU-I TRANS WALEY
　　Sent as a present from Amman
　　　　CHER 98　　　　　ECHO III 113　　　　HAP 16
　　　　M.P.W 97　　　　WAL.C.P 167

COCKS

The Cock, CHRISTINA ROSSETTI
　　'Kookoorookoo! Kookoorookoo!'
　　　　OX.V.J I 28

Cockcrow, EDWARD THOMAS
　　Out of the wood of thoughts that grow by night
　　　　FLA 40　　　　　KEY IV I 50　　　　THO.GR 23

Ditty, R. L. STEVENSON
　　The cock shall crow
　　　　OX.V.J I 9

I have a gentle cock, ANON
　　I have a gentle cock
　　　　OX.L.V 51　　　　OX.V.J I 9

I sometimes think, ANON
　　I sometimes think I'd rather crow
　　　　A.D.L 228　　　　B.P IV 60　　　　G.TR.P 228
　　　　KEY II 62　　　　PENG.YET 209　　WEALTH 17

COCOA

Lament for Cocoa, JOHN UPDIKE
　　The scum has come
　　　　HAP 79

COLOURS
Colours, CHRISTINA ROSSETTI
    What is pink? a rose is pink
        OX.V.J I 46   TREE II 81

COLUMBUS, CHRISTOPHER
How in all wonder Columbus got over, A. H. CLOUGH
    How in all wonder Columbus got over
        P.REM 67
There was an Indian, J. C. SQUIRE
    There was an Indian, who had known no change
        COME 379   P.F.P I 181   P.LIFE IV 50
        SCH.M.V 158

CONVERSATION
Talk, D. H. LAWRENCE
    I wish people, when you sit near them
        P.W 254

CORAL
Coral, CHRISTINA ROSSETTI
    O sailor, come ashore
        BL.J IV 26   OX.V.J I 49
The Coral Grove, J. G. PERCIVAL
    Deep in the wave is a coral grove
        OX.V.J IV 88

CORBIES
See **Ravens**

CORMORANTS
The Common Cormorant, ANON
    The common cormorant, or shag
        A.D.L 227   G.TR.P 223   MY 158
        PENG.COM 240   P.P.WIDE 41   P.TONG 123
        SPIR I

CORUNNA

The Burial of Sir John Moore at Corunna, C. WOLFE
    Not a drum was heard, not a funeral note
        CHER 342   COM 148   M.R.HAND 35
        P.F.P II 77   P.P.BRA 69   SPIR 84
        TOM.T.G 139

COUNTING RHYMES

See also *Chinese-Counting* OX.N.R 111–2

COUNTING RHYMES (UP)

Darlin', ANON
    Darlin' you can't love one
        PENG.A.F.S 90 (G,P)
    I'm ridin' on that New River Train
        A.F.B 74 (G)   S.T.S II 8 (G,P)

Green Grow the Rushes, Ho! ANON
    I'll sing you one, ho
        KEY III 48   OX.L.V 207   PEG II 102
        P.LIFE IV 80

Old Joe Braddle-Um, ANON
    Number one, number one
        MER 304

One, Two, ANON
    One, two / Buckle my shoe
        TOM.T.G 27

Over in the Meadow, ANON
    Over in the meadow, in the sand in the sun
        FAB.N.V 24

Ten Little Indian Boys, M. M. HUTCHINSON
    One little Indian boy making a canoe
        EX.T.TRA 10

This Old Man, ANON
    This old man, he played on
        P.LIFE II 62

The Twelve Days of Christmas, ANON
    On the first day of Christmas

B.P II 11	EX.T.H 53	FIRE.F.S 248 (P)
F.S.N.A 245 (G,B)	KEY III 47	MER 238
M.R.ON 104	OX.L.V 206	OX.N.R 198
OX.S.M.S I 14 (M)	P.LIFE III 56	P.P.FACT 40
PUF.N.R 184		

The Yule Days, ANON
    The king sent his lady on the first Yule day
        CHER 415

COUNTING RHYMES (DOWN)

One for the Frog, ANON
    Twelve huntsmen with horses and hounds
      MER 240   OX.V.J I 23   TREE I 50

Ten Little Injuns, ANON
    Ten little Injuns
      PUF.N.R 68

Ten Little Nigger Boys, ANON
    Ten little nigger boys went out to dine
      OX.N.R 193

COUNTING-OUT RHYMES
See FAB.N.V 19

COUNTRIES
See **Australia: England: France: Greece: Israel: Scotland: South Africa: U.S.A.**

COUNTRY LIFE

See also **Beanfields: Farmers: Farms: Farmworkers: Gamekeepers: Gipsies: Mole Catchers: Poachers: Ponds: Villages**

Afterwards, THOMAS HARDY
  When the Present has latched its postern

The Axe-Helve, ROBERT FROST
  I've known ere now an interfering branch

Buying Fuel, RICHARD CHURCH
  Now I come to the farmer about some logs

Come In, ROBERT FROST
  As I came to the edge of the woods

The Corbie and the Crow, ANON
  The corbie with his roupie throat

Evening Quatrains, CHARLES COTTON
  The day's grown old, the fainting sun

Farm Child, R. S. THOMAS
  Look at this village boy, his head is stuffed

Jack and Joan, THOMAS CAMPION
  Jack and Joan they think no ill

Leisure, W. H. DAVIES
> What is this life if, full of care
>> AN.METH 53   B.P III 78   COME 145
>> D.P.ROAD 17   JOY V   MOD 64
>> P.SING 159

The Looker-On, FRANK KENDON
> ... And ladders leaning against damson trees
>> PEG V 39

Lost in France, ERNEST RHYS
> He had the ploughman's strength
>> ALB I 135   PEG IV 87   P.TIME 95

Mending Wall, ROBERT FROST
> Something there is that does not love a wall
>> ECHO II 54   FRO.P 47   FRO.PENG 32
>> FRO.YOU 70   IRON II 44   M.P.W 37

The Merry Country Lad, N. BRETON
> Who can live in heart so gay
>> B.B.F 81

The Need of being versed in Country Things, ROBERT FROST
> The house had gone to bring again
>> FRO.P 300   FRO.PENG 152   PENG.E.V 417

The Pasture, ROBERT FROST
> I'm going out to clean the pasture spring
>> BL.J III 40   F.FEET 26   FRO.P I
>> FRO.PENG 19   FRO.YOU 20   M.R.FEEL 66
>> OX.V.J II 45   WEALTH 66

Pied Beauty, GERARD MANLEY HOPKINS
> Glory be to God for dappled things
>> A.D.L 203   D.P.F.F 184   G.TR.P 246
>> MOD 15   MY 182   PEG V 17
>> P.SING 33   R.R 165   SCH.M.V 71
>> THIS.W.D 112   WEALTH 63

COURTSHIP
See also **Lovers**

The Lover's Task, ANON
    Can you make me a cambric shirt?
        FAB.N.V 120   OX.N.R 196

My Man John, ANON
    My man John, what can the matter be
        KEY III 101

Oh no John, ANON
    On yonder hill there stands a creature
        G.TR.P 169   OX.S.M.J II 8 (M)

The Passionate Shepherd to his Love, CHRISTOPHER MARLOWE
    Come live with me and be my love
        PENG.E.V 31   R.R 137   WEALTH 82

Quoth John to Joan, ANON
    Quoth John to Joan, will thou have me
        COME 350

Rondeau, ANON
    By two black eyes my heart was won
        M.R.CHA 20

The Saucy Sailor, ANON
    Come, my own one, come my fond one
        KEY III 24

Scarborough Fair, ANON
    Where are you going? To Scarborough Fair?
        OX.L.V 286

Soldier, Soldier, ANON
    Soldier, soldier, won't you marry me
        D.P.JOU 98   EX.T.TRO 74   MER 142
        OX.L.V 363   OX.P.C 35   OX.S.M.J II 10 (M)
        PUF.N.R 176   S.N.W 38 (G,P)

Strawberry Fair, ANON
    As I was going to Strawberry Fair
        DRUM 59   MER 334

COWBOYS

Git along Little Dogies, ANON
> As I was walking one morning for pleasure
>> B.L.A.F.S 204 (G,P)   OX.S.M.J III 53 (M)   PENG.A.F.S 182
>> WHEEL I 106   F.S.N.A 372 (G,B)   (G,P)

Home on the Range, ANON
> O give me a home where the buffaloes roam
>> A.F.B 26 (G)   B.L.A.F.S 212 (G,P)   FIRE.F.S 164 (P)
>> S.N.W 19 (G,P)

The Streets of Laredo, ANON
> As I walked out in the streets of Laredo
>> A.F.B 41 (G)   B.L.A.F.S 206 (G,P)   CHER 137
>> IRON II 10   IVES 260 (G,P)   PEG II 70
>> PENG.A.F.S 184 (P,G) S.N.W 48 (G,P)   TREE III 89
>> WHEEL IV 126
> As I rode out by Tom Sherman's bar-room
>> FAB.BAL 242   F.S.N.A 384 (G,B)

COWS
See **Cattle**

COYOTES

Coyotes, BRET HARTE
> Blown out of the prairie in twilight and dew
>> KEY III 54   SPIR 44

CRABS

The Crabs, RICHARD LATTIMORE
> There was a bucket full of them. They spilled
>> PENG.AN 70
The Dead Crab, ANDREW YOUNG
> A rosy shield upon its back
>> R.R 53   YOU.P 93

CRANES

CREATION

CRICKET

CRICKETERS

CRICKETS

The Cricket, WILLIAM BLAKE
  Little inmate, full of mirth
    PENG.AN 77

CROCODILES

The Crocodile, ANON
  Now listen you landsmen unto me
    KEY I 45   PENG.M.C 258   P.TONG 95
    P.P.WIDE 14   P.W 24
A Ripple Song, RUDYARD KIPLING
  Once a ripple came to land
    KIP.INC 615

CROWS

The Carrion Crow, ANON
  A carrion crow sat on an oak
    OX.N.R 186
The Corbie and the Crow, ANON
  The corbie with his roupie throat
    P.P.TALK 61
I sometimes think, ANON
  I sometimes think I'd rather crow
    A.D.L 228   B.P IV 60   G.TR.P 228
    KEY II 62   PENG.YET 209   WEALTH 17
My Sister Jane, TED HUGHES
  And I say nothing—no, not a word
    HAP 16   HU.MEET 13

CRUCIFIXION

'And when he had scourged Jesus', W. R. RODGERS
  They took him out to die
    WEALTH 50

Woefully arrayed, ANON
> Woefully arrayed
>> CHER 385

CRUELTY

Peter Grimes (Part), G. CRABBE
> Now lived the youth in freedom, but debarred
>> WEALTH 110

CUCKOOS

See PUF.N.R 34

The Cuckoo, ANON
> The cuckoo is a pretty bird

B.B.F 51	CHER 49	IRON I 103
OX.S.M.J III 29 (M)	OX.S.M.S II 6 (M)	OX.V.J.I 29
TREE I 39		

The Cuckoo, ANON
> In April the cuckoo can sing her song by rote
>> KEY I 50

Cuckoo, Cuckoo, ANON
> Cuckoo, cuckoo, pray what do you do?

CHER 49	EX.T.TRA 22	FAB.N.V 76
OX.V.J I 29	P.LIFE II 51	PUF.V 16
TOM.T.G 56		

Cuckoo Song, RUDYARD KIPLING
> Tell it to the locked-up trees
>> KIP.INC 491

Cuckoos, ANDREW YOUNG
> When coltsfoot withers and begins to wear

KEY III 112	M.P.W 102	M.R.ON 62
PENG.AN 81	YOU.P 169	

Summer is y-cumin in, ANON
> Summer is y-cumin in

CHER 48	COM 57	C.S.B 110 (P)
KEY I 51	OX.E.V I	

CURSES

CYCLOPS

DAFFODILS

DANCING
See also **Ballet**

DANCING (LYRIC & DESCRIPTIVE)

My Dancing Day, ANON
   Tomorrow shall be my dancing day
       C.S.B 78 (P)   MER 296

The Fiddler of Dooney, W. B. YEATS
   When I play on my fiddle in Dooney
       A.D.L 127   AN.SPO I 166   EX.T.CH I 54
       FAB.C.V 41   M.R.CHA 10   OX.V.J II 26
       PEG II 99   P.LIFE III 42   YEA.P 82

Hornpipe, C. DAY LEWIS
   Now the peak of summer's past, the sky is overcast
       ALB II 104

Jig, C. DAY LEWIS
   That winter love spoke and we raised no objection
       ALB II 104   WEALTH 97

The Keel Row, ANON
   As I came through Sandgate
       P.P.TALK 12

The Lobster Quadrille, LEWIS CARROLL
   Will you walk a little faster? said a whiting to a snail
       B.B.F 197   CHER 29   D.P.WAY 45
       EX.T.TRO 53   MER 353   PENG.M.C 151
       P.LIFE II 26   P.P.FACT 18   P.REM 27
       P.TONG 185   V.F 30

Maypole Dance (1671), ANON
   Come lasses and lads, get leave of your dads
       D.P.JOU 94   OX.L.V 190   WEALTH 240

The Piper o' Dundee, ANON
   The piper came to our town
       OX.V.J II 82   PEG II 59   P.P.TALK 33

Polka, EDITH SITWELL
   Tra la la la—
       P.F.P II 20

Skip to my Lou, ANON
    Lou, Lou, skip to my Lou
        A.F.B 90 (G)   B.L.A.F.S 98 (G,P)   IVES 194 (G,P)
        S.N.W 37 (G,P)

Tarantella, H. BELLOC
    Do you remember an Inn
        BEL.S.V 130   COME 200   FAB.C.V 45
        JOY 97   P.F.P II 19   P.TONG 22
        SCH.M.V 6   WEALTH 4   WHEEL II 134

DANCING (NARRATIVE)

The Lost Shoe, WALTER DE LA MARE
    Poor little Lucy
        DE LA M.P II 142   EX.T.H 66   FAB.N.V 95

Off the Ground, WALTER DE LA MARE
    Three jolly Farmers
        DE LA M.P II 153   EX.T.CH 56   FAB.N.V 60
        OX.V.J II 66   P.F.P I 8   P.LIFE III 32
        P.P.FACT 22

DANGER

Good Taste, CHRISTOPHER LOGUE
    Travelling, a man met a tiger, so . . .
        DAWN 69   EV.M 83   HAP 63

DANIEL

The Daniel Jazz, VACHEL LINDSAY
    Darius the Mede was a king and a wonder
        CHER 143   KEY IV 28   LIN.P 159
        MY 59   P.F.P I 25   P.W 249
        WEALTH 168

DAUGHTERS

Daughters and Mothers, WALTER DE LA MARE
    Oh yes my dear, you have a mother
        JOY 145

Golden Bells, CHINESE TRANS WALEY
> When I was almost forty
>> WAL.C.P 136

DAVID
See also **Goliath**

Little David, ANON
> David was a shepherd boy,
>> OX.S.M.J III 43 (M)   PENG.A.F.S 126 (G,P)

DAWN
See also **Waking**

Break of Day, JOHN CLARE
> The lark he rises early
>> PEG III 11   TREE IV 100

Cock-crow, EDWARD THOMAS
> Out of the wood of thoughts that grow by night
>> FLA 40   KEY IV 150   THO.GR 23

Cock-crow Song, CHINESE TRANS WALEY
> In the eastern quarter dawn breaks, the stars flicker pale
>> KEY IV 149   WAL.C.P 115

Dawn, OSCAR WILDE
> The sky is laced with fitful red
>> KEY IV 149

Ditty, R. L. STEVENSON
> The cock shall crow
>> OX.V.J I 9

Early Astir, HERBERT READ
> Early, early I walked in the city
>> DAWN 94

Early Morn, W. H. DAVIES
> When I did wake this morn from sleep
>> COME 7

Hark! hark! the lark, WILLIAM SHAKESPEARE
   Hark ! hark ! the lark at heaven's gate sings
      CYMBELINE II iii 22   A.A 50   B.B.F 44
      CHER 264   OX.V.J II 18

Pippa Passes (Part), ROBERT BROWNING
   Faster and more fast
      PEG III 10

Sunrise, JOHN MILTON
   To hear the lark begin his flight
      KEY III 59

DEATH
See also **Funerals**

Ah, are you digging on my grave? THOMAS HARDY
   Ah, are you digging on my grave?
      HAR.PENG 97   HAR.SEL 30

The Door of Death, WILLIAM BLAKE
   The door of death is made of gold
      CHER 376

The Glories of our Blood and State, J. SHIRLEY
   The glories of our blood and state
      P.W 99   R.R 103

Holy Sonnet X, JOHN DONNE
   Death, be not proud, though some have called thee
      P.W 89   R.R 104

Like to the Falling of a Star, F. BEAUMONT
   Like to the falling of a star
      PEG IV 106

Proud Maisie, SIR WALTER SCOTT
   Proud Maisie is in the wood
      R.R 110

Transformations, THOMAS HARDY
   Portion of this yew
      HAR.PENG 143   THEME 23

DIRGES & LAMENTS

Anthem for Doomed Youth, WILFRED OWEN
     What passing-bells for these who die as cattle?

The Bonny Earl of Moray, ANON
     Ye Highlands and ye Lowlands

Burial Songs 1 *& 2,* CHINESE TRANS WALEY
     The dew on the garlic leaf
     The graveyard

David's Lament, THE BIBLE
     And David lamented with this lamentation

The Death and Burial of Cock Robin, ANON
     Who killed Cock Robin?

Fidele's Dirge, WILLIAM SHAKESPEARE
     Fear no more the heat o' the sun

The Flowers of the Forest, JANE ELLIOT
    I've heard them lilting at our ewe-milking
        OX.S.M.P 23 (M)   P.P.FAL 25   WEALTH 33

For Johnny, JOHN PUDNEY
    Do not despair
        DAY 75   M.R.HAND 42   WEALTH 49
        WHEEL IV 183

For the Fallen, LAURENCE BINYON
    With proud thanksgiving, a mother for her children
        MOD 57   SPIR 94

Full Fathom Five, WILLIAM SHAKESPEARE
    Full fathom five thy father lies
        TEMPEST I ii 394   AN.E.P 32   B.P II 53
        CHER 231   COM 187   D.P.WAY 119
        DRUM 39   ECHO I 24   FAB.C.V 268
        KEY III 118   MER 270   MY 29
        OX.V.J IV 89   PENG.E.V 67   P.F.P I 111
        P.P.BRA 47   P.REM 202   P.W 65
        THIS.W.D 83

Hymn to the Fallen, CHINESE TRANS WALEY
    We hold our flat shields, we wear our jerkins of hide
        WAL.C.P 35

In Memoriam (Easter 1915), EDWARD THOMAS
    The flowers left thick at nightfall in the wood
        THO.GR 87

In Plague Time, THOMAS NASHE
    Adieu, farewell earth's bliss
        AN.E.P 36   CHER 358   COME 261
        ECHO II 1   FAB.C.V 274   PENG.E.V 39
        P.P.WIDE 119   P.W 78   R.R 98
        WHEEL III 69

Li Fu-Jên, WU-TI TRANS WALEY
    The sound of her silk skirt has stopped
        WAL.C.P 42

Lost in France, ERNEST RHYS
> He had the ploughman's strength
>> ALB I 135   PEG IV 87   P.TIME 95

A Lyke-Wake Dirge, ANON
> This ae nighte, this ae nighte
>> BUN 236   CHER 366   COME 264
>> FAB.C.V 264   PEG V 104   P.P.FAL 47
>> PUF.V 204   P.W I   WHEEL III 34

O Death rock me on Sleep, ANNE BOLEYN (?)
> O Death rock me on sleep
>> CHER 357

Phylip Sparrow, JOHN SKELTON
> When I remember again
>> B.B.F I35

Song for Hedli Anderson, W. H. AUDEN
> Stop all the clocks, cut off the telephone
>> AUD.PENG 41   M.R.CHA 24   PEG V 53
>> WEALTH 48

The Streets of Laredo, ANON
> As I walked out in the streets of Laredo
>> A.F.B 41 (G)   B.L.A.F.S 206 (G,P)   CHER I37
>> IRON II IO   IVES 260 (G,P)   PEG II 70
>> PENG.A.F.S 184 (P,G)   S.N.W 48 (G,P)   TREE III 89
>> WHEEL IV 126
> As I rode out by Tom Sherman's bar-room
>> FAB.BAL 242   F.S.N.A 384 (G,B)

The Unquiet Grave, ANON
> The wind doth blow today, my love
>> BAL 262   COME 359   WEALTH 27

DISEASES
See **Illness**

DIVES AND LAZARUS

Dives and Lazarus, ANON
   As it fell out upon a day
      BAL I 77   ECHO III 12   FAB.BAL I 53

DOGS
See also **Puppies**

An Introduction to Dogs, OGDEN NASH
   The dog is man's best friend
      G.TR.P 38

Lone Dog, IRENE MCLEOD
   I'm a lean dog, a keen dog, a wild dog, a hunting dog
      A.D.L 177   AN.SPO I 134   EX.T.CH 19
      HAP 93   M.R.FEEL 40   PEG I 42
      PUF.V 42   TOM.T.G 68

Meditation, EZRA POUND
   When I carefully consider the curious habits of dogs
      P.REM 190   WEALTH 18

Mick, JAMES REEVES
   Mick my mongrel-O
      PUF.Q 80   TREE II 51

Sheep Dog Trials, C. DAY LEWIS
   A shepherd stands at one end of the arena
      HERE 50

Turkish Trench Dog, G. DEARMER
   Night held me as I crawled and scrambled near
      PEG III 46

DONKEYS
See also PUF.N.R 112–3 (for the youngest)

Asses, PADRAIC COLUM
   I know where I'd get
      OX.V.J III 13

The Donkey, G. K. CHESTERTON
  When fishes flew and forests walked

The Donkey's Fancy, J. H. FRERE
  A dingy donkey, formal and unchanged

Nicholas Nye, WALTER DE LA MARE
  Thistle and darnel and dock grew there

Wot cher! ANON
  Last week down our alley came a toff

DRAGONFLIES

The Dragon Fly, LORD TENNYSON
  Today I saw the dragon-fly

DRAGONS

The Dragon, from *The Faerie Queene* EDMUND SPENSER
  By this the dreadful beast drew nigh to hand

Fafnir, STEVIE SMITH
  In the quiet waters

Sir Eglamore, S. ROWLANDS
  Sir Eglamore that worthy knight

The Tale of Custard the Dragon, OGDEN NASH
    Belinda lived in a little white house
        G.TR.P 166   NA.P.B 80   WEALTH 204

DRAKE, SIR FRANCIS
See also **Armada**

Drake's Drum, H. NEWBOLT
    Drake he's in his hammock and a hundred miles away
        AN.SPO I 137   FAB.C.V 246   MOD 32
        SPIR 67   TOM.T.G 195   WEALTH I 52

Frankie's Trade, RUDYARD KIPLING
    Old Horn to All Atlantic said
        KIP.INC 644

Upon Sir Francis Drake's Return from his Voyage about the World
    (*c.* 1584), ANON
        'Sir Francis, Sir Francis, Sir Francis is come'
        C.MUSE 63

With Drake in the Tropics (*A.D. 1580*), RUDYARD KIPLING
    South and far south below the Line
        KIP.INC 699

DREAMS
See also **Nightmares**

Being on Duty all night in the Palace and dreaming of
    the Hsien–Yu temple, CHINESE TRANS WALEY
    At the western window I paused from writing rescripts
        WAL.C.P 112

What did I dream? ROBERT GRAVES
    What did I dream? I do not know
        GRA.FID 20

DRESS
The Well-Dressed Children, ROBERT GRAVES
    Here's flowery taffeta for Mary's new gown
        GRA.FID 47

DRINKING

Drinking, ABRAHAM COWLEY
    The thirsty earth soaks up the rain
        TREE IV 102   WEALTH 242   WHEEL III 77

Sound Advice, ANON
    Drink my good friend, drink with a noble heart
        KEY III 67

DRINKS
See **Ale: Cocoa**

DUCKS

Dilly, dilly, ANON
    Oh, what have you got for dinner, Mrs. Bond?
        MER 16   OX.N.R 171

Ducks, NORMAN AULT
    As I went down the village green
        EX.T.H 22

Ducks, F. W. HARVEY
    From troubles of the world I turn to ducks
        A.A 32   CH.GAR 64   D.P.ROAD 9
        DRUM 57   JOY 50   P.F.P I 41

Duck's Ditty, K. GRAHAME
    All along the backwater
        EX.T.H 23   FAB.N.V 78   F.Y.D 33
        M.R.FEEL 42   P.REM 17

New Duckling, A. NOYES
    'I want to be new' said the duckling
        A.A 35

Quack, WALTER DE LA MARE
    The duck is whiter than whey is
        EX.T.H 21

DUSTMEN

The Dustman, CLIVE SAMSON
　Every Thursday morning
　　BL.J I 28

EAGLES

The Eagle, LORD TENNYSON
　He clasps the crag with crooked hands

A.A 56	B.B.F 218	BL.J IV 50
COME 108	DRUM 58	EX.T.CH 18
FAB.C.V 89	G.TR.P 58	IRON I 11
KEY IV 70	OX.P.C 66	PENG.AN 99
P.F.P I 36	P.LIFE IV 18	P.P.OVER 19
THIS.W.D 120	WEALTH 58	

The Eagle, ANDREW YOUNG
　He hangs between his wings outspread

P.F.P I 36	P.LIFE IV 18	WEALTH 69
YOU.P 99		

EARTHQUAKES

Earthquake, JAMES KIRKUP
　An old man's flamingo-coloured kite
　　UNDER 47

EASTER

Easter, GEORGE HERBERT
　I got me flowers to straw thy way
　　COME 16

Easter Wings, GEORGE HERBERT
　Lord, who createdst man in wealth and store
　　KEY IV 63

EDEN
See **Eve**

EDUCATION
See also **Scholars: School: Schoolmasters**

Against Education, CHARLES CHURCHILL
>> Accursed the man, whom Fate ordains, in spite
>>> PEG V 73

Take Heart, Illiterates, J. RICHARDSON
>> For years a secret shame destroyed my peace
>>> PEG V 81

With Every Regret, MORRIS BISHOP
>> For many years the under-signed
>>> PENG.YET 135

EELS

Elvers, F. W. HARVEY
>> Up the Severn river from Lent to Eastertide
>>> DRUM 47

EGOISTS

warty bliggens the toad, DON MARQUIS
>> i met a toad
>>> EV.M 113   PEG V 113

ELDORADO

Eldorado, EDGAR ALLAN POE
>> Gaily bedight
>>> BL.J III 9   PEG II 25

ELEPHANTS

The Blind Men and the Elephant, J. SAXE
>> It was six men of Indostan
>>> A.A. 115   G.TR.P 200   KEY III 40
>>> OX.V.J II 63

Two Performing Elephants, D. H. LAWRENCE
>> He stands with his forefeet on a drum
>>> PEG IV 17

ELIZABETH I

The Looking Glass, RUDYARD KIPLING
> Queen Bess was Harry's daughter, stand forward partners all
> KIP.INC 590

A songe betwene the Quenes majestie and Englande, ANON
> Come over the born bessy
> C.MUSE 60

Tilbury Speech, ELIZABETH I
> My loving people, we have been persuaded
> AN.SPO II 51

EMOTIONS
See **Moods**

EMPERORS
See **Napoleon**

ENGINE DRIVERS AND FIREMEN

The Ballad of John Axon, EWAN MACCOLL
> John Axon was a railwayman
> KEY I 78

Career, DANIEL PETTIWARD
> I'd rather drive an engine than
> FAB.N.V 39

Casey Jones, ANON
> Come all you rounders that want to hear

B.L.A.F.S 266 (G,P)	D.P.WAY 34	EX.T.CH 164
FIRE.F.S 142 (P)	F.S.N.A 564 (G,B)	IRON II 77
KEY I 84	M.M.A 23	M.R.ON 20
OX.L.V 453	OX.P.C 76	OX.V.J IV 25
PEG II 78	P.F.P I 156	P.P.WIDE 68
P.TONG 17	SPIR 58	S.T.S I 12 (G)

> On a Sunday morning it begins to rain
> B.L.A.F.S 264 (G,P)
> Some folks say Casey Jones can't run
> PENG.A.F.S 216 (G,P)

The Fireman's Calypso, EWAN MACCOLL
> You give her water
>> KEY II 26

The Fireman's not for me, EWAN MACCOLL
> Come all you young maidens take warning from me
>> S.T.S I 40 (G)

ENGINEERS

Engineers, J. GARTHWAITE
> Pistons, valves and wheels and gears
>> FAB.N.V 41

McAndrew's Hymn, RUDYARD KIPLING
> Lord, thou has made this world below
> the shadow of a dream
>> A.B.L.P 646   KIP.INC 120

ENGINES

Thursday's Child (Part), CHRISTOPHER FRY
> You are living against a pulse of steel
>> PEG V 96

ENGLAND

A Charm, RUDYARD KIPLING
> Take of English earth as much
>> JOY 3   KIP.INC 492

Jerusalem, WILLIAM BLAKE
> And did those feet in ancient time
>> AN.E.P 77   B.P IV 39   CH.GAR 75
>> D.P.F.F 187   EX.T.CH 25   P.W 142

Puck's Song, RUDYARD KIPLING
> See you the dimpled track that runs
>> BL.J IV 28   COM I 11   D.P.JOU 104
>> FAB.C.V 129   KIP.INC 480   P.LIFE IV 72
>> P.P.BRA 93

St. George and the Dragon (Part), ANON
Here stand I, Saint George;
COM 160

This England, WILLIAM SHAKESPEARE
This royal throne of kings, this sceptred isle
RICHARD II II i 40–50   M.R.CHA 5

ENGLAND: HISTORY
See also **Kings & Queens: War: Wars**

ENGLAND: HISTORY (PRE-ROMAN)

The River's Tale, RUDYARD KIPLING
Twenty bridges from Tower to Kew
KEY III 78   KIP.INC 689

ENGLAND: HISTORY (ROMAN)

Over the heather, W. H. AUDEN
Over the heather the wet wind blows
AUD.PENG 46   DAWN 43   MY 79
PEG V 95   PENG.COM 302   WEALTH 250

Roman Road, A. G. PRYS-JONES
This is the way the Romans came
AN.SPO I 142

ENGLAND: HISTORY (SAXONS AND NORMANS)

The Pirates in England (*Saxon Invasion A.D. 400–600*),
RUDYARD KIPLING
When Rome was rotten-ripe to her fall
KEY III 20   KIP.INC 691

Sir Richard's Song (*A.D. 1066*), RUDYARD KIPLING
I followed my Duke ere I was a lover
KIP.INC 487

ENGLAND: HISTORY (MEDIAEVAL)
See also **Agincourt: Runnymede**

King Henry Fifth's Conquest of France, ANON
>As our king lay musing on his bed
>>BAL 464

ENGLAND: HISTORY (MARY TUDOR)

The Martyrdom of Bishop Farrar, TED HUGHES
>Bloody Mary's venomous flames can curl
>>THEME 82

ENGLAND: HISTORY (ELIZABETH I)
See also **Armada: Calais: Drake, Sir Francis: Elizabeth I: Grenville, Sir Richard**

The Looking Glass, RUDYARD KIPLING
>Queen Bess was Harry's daughter. Stand forward partners all
>>KIP.INC 590

In Time of Plague, THOMAS NASHE
>Adieu, farewell earth's bliss

AN.E.P 36	CHER 358	COME 261
ECHO II I	FAB.C.V 274	PENG.E.V 39
P.P.WIDE I19	P.W 78	R.R 98
WHEEL III 69		

Lord Willoughby (c. 1586), ANON
>The fifteen day of July
>>C.MUSE 64

ENGLAND: HISTORY (CHARLES I)
See **Cavaliers: Charles I**

ENGLAND: HISTORY (CHARLES II)
See also **Charles II**

London, sad London, ANON
>What wants thee that thou art in this sad taking?
>>P.REM I37

The Vicar of Bray, ANON
    In good King Charles' golden days
        OX.L.V 260   P.P.FAL 91

When the King enjoys his own again, MARTIN PARKER
    What Booker can prognosticate
        OX.L.V 150

ENGLAND: HISTORY (JAMES II)

The Song of the Western Men, R. S. HAWKER
    A good sword and a trusty hand
        MER 225   M.R.ON 11   OX.S.M.J III 8 (M)
        P.P.FACT 39

ENGLAND: HISTORY (WILLIAM & MARY)
See also **Benbow**

A New Song of a Pudding (1688), ANON
    Good People, come buy
        C.MUSE 117

ENGLAND: HISTORY (THE GEORGES)
See also **Corunna: Nelson: Trafalgar**

Poor Honest Men (*A.D. 1800*), RUDYARD KIPLING
    Your jar of Virginny
        KIP.INC 537

A Smuggler's Song, RUDYARD KIPLING
    If you wake at midnight and hear a horse's feet

B.P IV 47	D.P.JOU 72	EX.T.CH 117
KEY II 94	KIP.INC 636	M.R.ON 18
OX.V.J II 10	OX.P.C 52	PEG I 62
P.LIFE III 92	P.P.TALK 20	P.SING 78
SPIR 22		

We be the King's Men, THOMAS HARDY
We be the King's men hale and hearty

COME 175	DRUM 15	EX.T.CH 105
MER 346	M.R.FEEL 27	TOM.T.G 137

ENGLAND: HISTORY (VICTORIA)
See also **Balaclava**

Fourpence a Day, ANON
The ore's a-waiting in the tubs, the snows upon the fell
S.T.S I 51 (G)

ENGLISHMEN

The Englishman, G. K. CHESTERTON
St. George he was for England
M.M.A 74

EPIPHANY

The Journey of the Magi, T. S. ELIOT
A cold coming we had of it

ALB II 47	ECHO III I	EL.P 107
EV.M 103	FAB.C.V 359	FAB.M.V 123
IRON II 8	MOD 150	P.TONG II I
P.W 260	SCH.M.V 45	TW.N 132
WEALTH 294	WHEEL III 158	

On the Morning of Christ's Nativity (Part), JOHN MILTON
See how from far upon the eastern road
CHER 426

EPITAPHS

Cover me Over, RICHARD EBERHART
Cover me over, clover
R.R 144

Epitaph, HENRY WOTTON
He first deceased

ECHO II 25	WEALTH 31

Epitaph, RUDYARD KIPLING
    I could not dig; I dared not rob
        KIP.INC 383   R.R 168

Epitaph to the Four Husbands of Miss Ivy Saunders, ANON
    Here lie my husbands, one, two, three
        WEALTH 17

An Epitaph upon a Young Married Couple, R. CRASHAW
    To these, whom Death again did wed
        ECHO III 143

Five Epitaphs, VARIOUS
        R.R 97

His Being was in Her alone, SIR PHILIP SIDNEY
    His being was in her alone
        THEME 113

Requiem, R. L. STEVENSON
    Under the wide and starry sky
        MY 177   SPIR 104

Upon a Child, ROBERT HERRICK
    Here a pretty baby lies
        MY 172

Written on the Night before his Execution, SIR WALTER RALEGH
    Even such is Time, that takes in trust
        CHER 381   OX.V.J IV 91   R.R 100
        WEALTH 286

ESKIMOS

Angutivaun Taina: Song of the Returning Hunter
    RUDYARD KIPLING
        Our gloves are stiff with the frozen blood
        KIP.INC 648

EVE

Eve, RALPH HODGSON
    Eve, with her basket was
        COME 485   MOD 76   MY 46
        WEALTH 158

EVENING

Evening, from *Paradise Lost*, JOHN MILTON
    Now came still Evening on, and Twilight grey
        PEG III 10

Evening Quatrains, CHARLES COTTON
    The day's grown old, the fainting sun
        CHER 450

Sowing, EDWARD THOMAS
    It was a perfect day
        A.D.L 264   OX.V.J IV 84   PEG IV 49
        SCH.M.V 168   THO.GR 29

Summer Evening, JOHN CLARE
    Crows crowd croaking overhead
        TREE IV 100

Summer Evening, WALTER DE LA MARE
    The sandy cat by the farmer's chair
        TREE II 15

Time to go Home, JAMES REEVES
    Time to go home
        OX.V.J II 92

EXCUSES

Explanation on Coming Home Late, R. HUGHES (aged 7)
    We went down to the river's brink
        THIS.W.D 13

EXPLORERS
See **Columbus: Drake**

EXPLORING
Away out on the Mountain, KELLY HARRELL
  I'll pack my grip for a farewell trip
    ECHO III 43

The Far-Farers, R. L. STEVENSON
  The broad sun
    OX.V.J III 52

Travel, R. L. STEVENSON
  I should like to rise and go
    FAB.C.V 100   G.TR.P 263   M.R.HAND 21
    PEG I 52

FABLES
The Donkey's Fancy, J. H. FRERE
  A dingy donkey, formal and unchanged
    KEY III 37
Haec Fabula Docet, ROBERT FROST
  A Blindman by the name of La Fontaine
    FRO.P 561   FRO.PENG 246

FACTORIES
Factory windows are always broken, VACHEL LINDSAY
  Factory windows are always broken
    LIN.P 266   P.F.P II 110   R.R 68

FAIRIES
See also **Robin Goodfellow**
Berries, WALTER DE LA MARE
  There was an old woman
    EX.T.TRO 80   M.R.ON 76   P.SING 88

The Fairies, W. ALLINGHAM
  Up the airy mountain
    B.P II 40   CHER I 57   CH.GAR 39
    COM 198   COME I 22   EX.T.H 76
    FAB.C.V 209   F.Y.D 99   MER 97
    P.P.OVER 10   PUF.V 190   TOM.T.G 50

A Fairy Song, JOHN LYLY
    Pinch him, pinch him black and blue
        THIS.W.D 32

Hie Away, SIR WALTER SCOTT
    Hie away, hie away
        MY 149

Now the Hungry Lion roars, WILLIAM SHAKESPEARE
    Now the hungry lion roars
        MIDSUMMER NIGHT'S DREAM V ii   AN.SPO I 149
        PEG I 100   THIS.W.D 40

Over hill, over dale, WILLIAM SHAKESPEARE
    Over hill, over dale
        MIDSUMMER NIGHT'S DREAM II i 2   OX.V.J I 62
        THIS.W.D 75   TOM.T.G 113

The Stolen Child, W. B. YEATS
    Where dips the rocky highland
        AN.SPO I 167

Where the bee sucks, WILLIAM SHAKESPEARE
    Where the bee sucks
        TEMPEST V i 88   CH.GAR 20   COME 121
        DRUM 75   ECHO I 99   EX.T.TRO 75
        MER 259   M.R.HAND 7   MY 26
        OX.S.M.P 47 (M)   P.P.OVER 50   P.W 65
        THIS.W.D 76   TREE I 19

You spotted snakes, WILLIAM SHAKESPEARE
    You spotted snakes with double tongue
        MIDSUMMER NIGHT'S DREAM II ii 9   B.B.F 165
        B.P IV 94   CH.GAR 18   D.P.JOU 103
        EX.T.CH 28   F.FEET I 57   G.TR.P 297
        MER 367   MY 27   OX.V.J II 75
        P.LIFE II 78   P.REM 40   P.SING 50
        THIS.W.D 37   TREE II 32

FAIRS
See also **Roundabouts**

Back to the Fair, JOHN ARLOTT
>   Tonight, a cloud-rimmed flowering of the air
>   ALB I I

Flight of the Roller Coaster, R. SOUSTER
>   'One more round should do it' the man confided
>   PEG V 12

Strawberry Fair, ANON
>   As I was going to Strawberry Fair
>   DRUM 59   MER 334

FALLING ASLEEP
See also **Lullabies**

Falling Asleep, S. SASSOON
>   Voices moving about in the quiet house
>   OX.V.J III 56

FAMILIES
See also HU.MEET throughout
See also **Brothers: Daughters: Fathers: Grandfathers: Mothers: Sisters: Uncles**

Family Court, OGDEN NASH
>   One would be in less danger
>   NA.P.B 88

FAMOUS PEOPLE
See also **Clerihews**
See also **Acrobats: Emperors: Explorers: Generals: Highwaymen: Kings and Queens: Painters: Poets: Sailors**

Let us now praise famous men, THE APOCRYPHA
>   Let us now praise famous men
>   ECCLESIASTICUS xliv   CHER 376
>   D.P.F.F 186   ECHO III 85   PEG IV 65

FANTASY
See also **Animals, Fantastic: Mystery: Tales, Tall**

I saw a fishpond, ANON
    I saw a fishpond all on fire
        BL.J III 56   CHER I 53   KEY I 29
        OX.N.R 136   PUF.N.R 106

I saw a pack of cards, ANON
    I saw a pack of cards gnawing a bone
        PUF.N.R 107

The Westminster Drollery (1671) (Part), ANON
    I saw a peacock with a fiery tail
        B.P IV 15   CHER I 54   COM 117
        COME 294   G.TR.P 228   MER 282
        MY 22   OX.N.R 141   PENG.COM 218
        P.P.FACT 20   PUF.N.R 106

*   *   *

If all the seas, ANON

    If all the seas were one sea
        BL.J I 53   MER 38   P.LIFE I 15
If all the world (1641), ANON
    If all the world were paper
        A.D.L 223

*   *   *

Flight of the Roller Coaster, R. SOUSTER

    'One more round should do it' the man confided
        PEG V 12

I'll sail upon the Dog-Star, THOMAS DURFEY
    I'll sail upon the dog-star
        COM 175

The Road to Roundabout, G. K. CHESTERTON
    Some say that Guy of Warwick
        CHES.P 214   JOY 194

The Rolling English Road, G. K. CHESTERTON
    Before the Roman came to Rye or out to Severn strode

CHES.P 203	D.P.F.F 79	FAB.C.V 292
P.P.WIDE 9		

Romance, W. J. TURNER
    When I was but thirteen or so

A.D.L 140	COME 375	D.P.ROAD 89
PAT 193	PEG II 106	P.F.P II 5
P.TIME 80	PUF.V 209	SCH.M.V 176
THIS.W.D 135	WEALTH 12	

The Song of the Mad Prince, WALTER DE LA MARE
    Who said 'Peacock Pie'?

DE LA M.CH 127	DE LA M.P II 249	FAB.C.V 282
IRON II 129	MY 32	P.P.OVER 62
P.TONG 184	R.R 115	

Still the dark Forest, W. H. AUDEN
    Still the dark forest, quiet the deep

EX.T.TRO 88	OX.V.J I 71

Tartary, WALTER DE LA MARE
    If I were Lord of Tartary

DE LA M.P II 7	EX.T.TRO 84	G.TR.P 105
MOD 80	P.LIFE IV 92	TREE IV 93

There is an Inn, J. R. R. TOLKIEN
    There is an inn, a merry old inn

        KEY II 45

Tom o' Bedlam's Song, ANON
    The moon's my constant mistress

ECHO II 63	FAB.C.V 186	P.P.WIDE 85

Welsh Incident, ROBERT GRAVES
    But that was nothing to what things came out

ALB I 77	COM 121	GRA.P 108
GRA.PENG 86	PEG IV 22	PENG.C.V 129
P.F.P II 222	R.R 178	WEALTH 196

FARMERS

The Farmer is the Man, ANON
> When the farmer comes to town
>> A.F.B 57 (G)   F.S.N.A 132 (G,B)

The Times have Altered (c. 1820), ANON
> Come all you swaggering farmers, whoever you may be
>> C.MUSE 179

FARMING

See **Barley: Beanfields: Country Life: Farmworkers:
Farmyards: Harvest: Haystacks: Mowing: Ploughing:
Reaping, See Harvest: Scarecrows: Sowing: Tractors**

FARMWORKERS

See also **Carters**

Cynddylan on a Tractor, R. S. THOMAS
> Ah, you should see Cynddylan on a tractor
>> DAWN 78   HAP 26   HERE 18
>> WHEEL IV 188

The Death of the Hired Man, ROBERT FROST
> Mary sat musing on the lamp flame at the table
>> FRO.P 49   FRO.PENG 34   KEY IV 152

The Farmer's Boy, ANON
> The sun went down beyond yon hill, across yon dreary moor
>> DRUM 83

'Twas early one morning, ANON
> 'Twas early one morning at the break of the day
>> COM 25

FARMYARDS

The Farmyard, ANON
> Up was I on my father's farm
>> TREE II 16

FESTIVALS
See **Christmas: Easter: Epiphany: May Day: New Year**

FIDDLES
See **Violins**

FIGHTING

Bill 'Awkins, RUDYARD KIPLING
    'As anybody seen Bill 'Awkins?
        KIP.INC 436

The Combat, EDWIN MUIR
    It was not meant for human eyes
        PENG.C.V 93   TW.N 136

Emperors of the Island, DANNIE ABSE
    There is the story of a deserted island
        DAWN 87   DAY 99

The fox-coloured pheasant enjoyed his peace, P. LEVI
    The fox-coloured pheasant enjoyed his peace
        DAWN 36

Johnny Wayne and Randy Scott, ROBERT SERVICE
    Johnny Wayne and Randy Scott
        M.R.ON 44

FINANCIERS

Thrushes, HUMBERT WOLFE
    The City Financier
        B.P II 49   OX.V.J III 29   P.LIFE III 72

FIREMEN
See **Engine Drivers**

FIREMEN (FIRE-FIGHTING)

Fire Down Below, ANON
    Fire in the galley, fire down below
        TREE I 22

The Firemen's Ball (Part), VACHEL LINDSAY
>   Give the engines room
>   LIN.P 319   M.R.ON 5

The Smithfield Market Fire, F. DALLAS
>   The coldest day in all the year
>   WEALTH 172

The Streets of Laredo, LOUIS MACNIECE
>   O early one morning I walked out like Agag
>   (for model, see **Cowboys**)
>   CHER 309   FLA 111   RIS 112

FIREWORKS

Firework Night, E. SIMPSON
>   The sky is filled with sparks and flames
>   EV.M 33

Fireworks, JAMES REEVES
>   They rise like sudden fiery flowers
>   BL.J III 6   P.LIFE II 56   PUF.Q 59

Gunpowder Plot, VERNON SCANNELL
>   For days those curious cardboard buds have lain
>   FLA 172

FISHERMEN

Caller Herrin', LADY NAIRNE
>   Who'll buy my caller herrin'?
>   OX.S.M.P 44 (M)

FISHES & SEA CREATURES
See also **Crabs: Eels: Flying Fish: Herring: Kraken: Leviathan: Lobsters: Mermaids: Minnows: Octopi: Oysters: Pike: Sea Monsters: Seals: Sharks: Turtles: Whales**

Alas, Alack, WALTER DE LA MARE
>   Ann, Ann!
>   DE LA M.P. II 111   FAB.N.V 64   MER 88
>   PEG I 99   TREE I 59

Clarence's Dream, WILLIAM SHAKESPEARE
Methought that I had broken from the Tower
RICHARD III I iv 9-33   CHER 229
PEG.V 107   P.W 70

The Fish, RUPERT BROOKE
Those silent waters seave for him
PEG III 39

The Fish and the Man, LEIGH HUNT
You strange, astonished-looking, angle-faced
PEG III 43   PENG.AN 112

Heaven, RUPERT BROOKE
Fish (fly-replete) in depth of June
A.D.L 167   D.P.F.F 30   PAT 43
P.P.BRA 65   P.TIME 62   WHEEL I 147

The Water Zoo, E. V. KNOX
Today I have seen all I wish
PEG IV 18

FISHING
See also **Shrimping: Whaling**

The Boy Fishing, E. J. SCOVELL
I am cold and alone
OX.V.J III 37   THIS.W.D 14

The Fish, ELIZABETH BISHOP
I caught a tremendous fish
PENG.AN 114

The Fisher, W. RENTON
The fisher is holding his handle-net
WEALTH 216

Morning Herring, NAOMI MITCHISON
It will be morning soon
OX.V.J IV 86

Some Old Rhymes about Fish and Fishing, ANON
>Watch, barrel, watch
>>OX.V.J III 27–8

Winds for Fishing, ANON
>When the wind is in the North
>>TREE I 27

FLIES

The Blue-Tailed Fly, ANON
>When I was young I used to wait
>>A.F.B 12 (G)   F.S.N.A 505 (G,B)
>>PENG.A.F.S 104 (G,P)   R.R 176

The Fly, WALTER DE LA MARE
>How large unto the tiny fly
>>A.A 86   B.B.F 118   DE LA M.CH 37
>>DE LA M.P II 13   DRUM 76   EX.T.H 19
>>F.FEET 186   OX.V.J I 56   PENG.AN 119
>>P.P.BELL 41   TREE I 61

The Fly, WILLIAM BLAKE
>Little fly
>>BLA.P 72   BLA.PENG 48   PENG.AN 118

FLOOD, THE
See **Noah**

FLOODS

By the Tyne, ANDREW YOUNG
>What foolish birds were they
>>YOU.P 98

The Floating Island, RUTH MILLER
>Down the glutted river's throat
>>P.SING 193

Flood, CHINESE TRANS WALEY
>The lingering clouds, rolling, rolling
>>WAL.C.P 107

The High Tide on the Coast of Lincolnshire, J. INGELOW
　The old mayor climbed to the belfry tower
　　　SPIR I 50

FLOWERS
See also **Chrysanthemums: Daffodils: Gentians: Marigolds: Roses: Thistles**

The Broken-hearted Gardener, ANON
　I'm a broken-hearted gardener and don't know what to do
　　　CHER 271

Daphnis to Ganymede, RICHARD BARNFIELD
　If thou wilt come and dwell with me at home
　　　THIS.W.D 57

FLYCATCHERS
The Flycatcher, SYLVIA LYND
　That is the flycatcher's wing beneath the eaves
　　　KEY IV 69

FLYING-FISH
The Flattered Flying-Fish, E. V. RIEU
　Said the shark to the flying-fish over the phone
　　　B.P III 3 I　　　　PUF.Q I22

FOG
Fog, CARL SANDBURG
　The fog comes / On little cat feet
　　　EV.M 43　　　　G.TR.P 255　　　　M.R.CHA 43

The Fog, W.H. DAVIES
　I saw the fog grow thick
　　　BL.J III 5　　　　KEY IV I28　　　　PEG I I03

Fog, CROSBIE GARSTIN
　Over the oily swell it heaved, it rolled
　　　PEG III 3 I　　　　R.R 38

FOOD

Bread and Cherries, WALTER DE LA MARE
   Cherries, ripe cherries
         DE LA M.P II 120   EX.T.TRA 76   OX.V.J I 13

Crusty Bread, E. V. LUCAS
   The country is the place for milk
         M.R.FEEL 64

Food and Drink, LOUIS UNTERMEYER
   Why has our poetry eschewed
         PEG V 26

Hot Cake, SHU HSI TRANS WALEY
   Winter has come; fierce is the cold
         A.D.L 101   IRON II 68   WAL.C.P 86

Miss T., WALTER DE LA MARE
   It's a very odd thing
         DE LA M.CH 63   DE LA M.P II 129   IRON I 16
         TREE II 23   V.F 52

One Fishball, ANON
   A wretched man walked up and down
         PENG.YET 39

Pancakes, CHRISTINA ROSSETTI
   Mix a pancake
         OX.V.J I 11

Robbin the Bobbin, ANON
   Robbin the Bobbin whose surname was Ben
         BL.J.I 9   TREE II 12

FOOTBALL

Football Crazy, ANON
   I have a favourite brother and his Christian name is Paul
         S.T.S II 22 (G,P)

FOREIGNERS

French and English, THOMAS HOOD
Never go to France
TREE IV 86

The Little Black Boy, WILLIAM BLAKE
My mother bore me in the southern wild

BLA.P 67	BLA.PENG 28	CH.GAR 172
COM 40	COME 22	MER 291
P.REM 34	P.W 139	WHEEL II 71

We and They, RUDYARD KIPLING
Father and Mother and Me
KIP.INC 743

FORESTERS

The Jolly Forester, ANON
I am a jolly forester
OX.V.J III 41

FOXES

The False Fox, ANON
The false fox came unto our croft
CHER 113

Four Little Foxes, LEE SANNETT
Speak gently, spring, and make no sudden sound
PEG I 44

The Fox, ANON
A fox jumped up ...
The fox went out one winter's night, etc.

A.F.B 80 (G)	BAL 749	BL.J II 13
D.P.JOU 17	EX.T.H 50	G.TR.P 32
IVES 28 (G,P)	KEY II 117	MER 109, 111
M.R.FEEL 86	MY 57	OX.N.R 190
OX.P.C 114	P.F.P I 52	P.LIFE III 88
PUF.V 48	S.T.S I 22 (G)	TOM.T.G 78
TREE III 18		

E

Reynard the Fox (Part), JOHN MASEFIELD
    The fox was strong, he was full of running
        PENG.AN I 19
    The pure clean air came sweet to his lungs
        AN.SPO I 44
    And here as he ran to the huntsman's yelling
        M.M.A 50
    For a minute he ran and heard no sound
        TW.N 99
    Two hundred yards and the trees grew taller
        KEY III 91

Three Little Foxes, A. A. MILNE
    Once upon a time there were three little foxes
        B.P I 47   FAB.N.V 90

The Vixen, JOHN CLARE
    Among the woods with ivy hung
        BL.J IV 52   TREE III 37

FRANCE
See also **Napoleon**

La Marseillaise, ROUGET DE LISLE
    Ye sons of France awake to glory
    Allons, enfants de la patrie
        FIRE.F.S 223 (P)

'FREEDOM SONGS' (U.S.A)

Go Down, Moses, ANON
    When Israel was in Egypt's land
        B.L.A.F.S 372 (G,P)   FIRE.F.S 316 (P)   PENG.A.F.S 138
                                                        (P,G)

Great Day, ANON
    Great day
        PENG.A.F.S 140 (G,P)

Guide my feet while I run this race, ANON
    Never turn back while I run this race
        W.S.O 102 (G)

I'm so glad, ANON
    I'm so glad I'm fighting to be free
        W.S.O 71 (G)

Oh Mary don't you weep, ANON
    If I could I surely would
        A.F.B 78 (G)

One Man's Hands, ALEX COMFORT AND PETE SEEGER
    One man's hands can't tear a prison down
        W.S.O 79 (G)

We shall not be Moved, ANON
    We shall not, we shall not be moved
        A.F.B 38 (G)   W.S.O 71 (G)

We shall overcome, ANON
    We shall overcome
        W.S.O 11 (G)

FROGS

The Frog, H. BELLOC
    Be kind and tender to the frog
        BEL.PUF 108   M.R.ON 58

The Frog, JOHN BUNYAN
    The frog by nature is both damp and cold
        ECHO III 122

The love-sick Frog, ANON
    A frog he would a-wooing go
        OX.N.R 172

The Two Frogs, ANON
    Two frogs fell into a milk-pail deep
        BL.J II 53

FROST & ICE
See also **Skating**

The Backs in February, JOHN PRESS
    Winter's keen blade has stripped
        PEG IV 48

Hard Frost, ANDREW YOUNG
    Frost called to water 'Halt!'
        KEY IV 73   M.CENT 27   PAT 18
        YOU.P 206

Ice, WALTER DE LA MARE
    The North Wind sighed
        DE LA M.CH 53   EX.T.CH 32   P.LIFE IV 30
        UNDER 91

The Ice Cart, W. W. GIBSON
    Perched on my city office-stool
        AN.METH 87   AN.SPO I 115   D.P.F.F 77
        M.R.CHA 112   PEG II 2   P.F.P II 41
        P.SING 73   SCH.M.V 59   WHEEL II 139

When icicles hang by the wall,   WILLIAM SHAKESPEARE
    When icicles hang by the wall
        LOVE'S LABOURS LOST V ii 920   A.A 46
        B.B.F 109   CHER 392   CH.GAR 20
        COM 76   COME 246   D.P.JOU 106
        ECHO I 96   FAB.C.V 56   F.Y.D 57
        IRON I 50   KEY.I 75   MER 348
        M.R.HAND 6   OX.P.C 98   OX.V.J II 59
        PAT 21   P.F.P I 44   P.LIFE II 58
        P.P.TALK 78   PUF.V 128   THIS.W.D 72

FRUIT
See also **Apples: Cherries: Lychees**

Goblin Market (Part), CHRISTINA ROSSETTI
    Morning and evening
        P.F.P II 198   P.P.OVER 82

FUNERALS

The Choirmaster's Burial, THOMAS HARDY
   He often would ask us
      HAR.PENG 156   TW.N 56

GAMEKEEPERS

The Gallows, EDWARD THOMAS
   There was a weasel lived in the sun
      ECHO I 78   KEY III 144   M.R.CHA.80
      P.P.FAL 37   THO.GR 44   WHEEL III 143
The Grey Squirrel, HUMBERT WOLFE
   Like a small grey
      PENG.AN 294
The Keeper, ANON
   The keeper did a shooting go
      A.F.B 59 (G)   MER 118   OX.S.M.J II 26 (M)

GAMES

See **Boats, Paper: Hide and Seek: Hobbyhorses: Physical
   Activity: Sport**

GARDENERS

The Broken-Hearted Gardener, ANON
   I'm a broken-hearted gardener, and don't know what to do
      CHER 271

GARDENS

The Garden, ANDREW MARVELL
   What wondrous life is this I lead
      CHER 268

GEESE

The Goose, LORD TENNYSON
   I knew an old wife lean and poor
      KEY II 118   OX.V.J III 44

Grey Goose and Gander, ANON
> Grey goose and gander
>> B.B.F 195   CHER 174   MER 113

The Old Grey Goose, ANON
> Go and tell Aunt Nancy
>> B.L.A.F.S 16 (G,P)   CHER 108   IVES 175 (G,P)
>> KEY II 118   OX.P.C 154   PENG.A.F.S 95 (G,P)

Something told the Wild Geese, RACHEL FIELD
> Something told the wild geese
>> MY 114

GENERALS
See **Booth: Hannibal: Napoleon**

GENTIANS
Bavarian Gentians, D. H. LAWRENCE
> Not every man has gentians in his house
>> LAW.PENG 121   PEG.V 25

GHOSTS (LYRIC & DESCRIPTIVE)

Dicky, ROBERT GRAVES
> Mother: Oh, what a heavy sigh!
>> GRA.FID 26

The Fause Knight upon the Road, ANON
Meet on the Road
> O where are ye gaun?
>> BUN 84   COME 334   EX.T.H 29
>> FAB.C.V 105   KEY IV 92   MER 122
>> M.M.A 30   OX.L.V 98   OX.P.C 84
>> OX.V.J II 33   P.F.P I 56   P.TONG 99
>> PUF.V 205   TREE IV 116

The Ghost in the Garden, OSBERT SITWELL
> For clanking and lank
>> OX.V.J III 78

The Ghosts, T. L. PEACOCK
> In life three ghostly friars were we
>> MY 35

Wae's Me, ANON
> Wae's me! Wae's me!

B.P III 70	BUN 84	COM 140
COME 332	MER 346	M.M.A 44
OX.L.V 185	PEG II 69	P.P.OVER 48
PUF.V 186	TREE III 55	

GHOSTS (NARRATIVE)

The Alice Jean, ROBERT GRAVES
> One moonlight night a ship drove in
>> GRA.FID 54

The Choirmaster's Burial, THOMAS HARDY
> He often would ask us
>> HAR.PENG 156   TW.N 56

The Crooked Pear Tree Hill, L. CLARK
> Under the hill there burns a fire
>> M.M.A 25

Miss Bailey's Ghost, ANON
> A captain bold in Halifax who dwelt in country quarters
>> OX.L.V 404

Shooting of his Dear, ANON
> Come all you young people who handle a gun
>> M.M.A 29   OX.L.V 370

The Wife of Usher's Well, ANON
> There lived a wife at Usher's Well

BAL 263	BUN 37	CHER 134
COME 445	FAB.BAL 58	M.M.A 87
M.R.CHA 107	OX.V.J IV 93	PEG I 92
P.F.P I 145	P.LIFE IV 48	P.TONG 166
P.W 2	TOM.T.G 171	

GIANTS

Grim, WALTER DE LA MARE
  Beside the blaze of forty fires
      DE LA M.CH 94   DE LA M.P II 207
      TREE III 51

Gulliver in Lilliput, ALEXANDER POPE
  From his nose
      TREE III 85

GIPSIES

The Earl of Cashan's Lady, ANON
  There came seven gipsies on a day
      P.P.OVER 37

Gipsies, JOHN CLARE
  The gipsies seek wide sheltering woods again
      DRUM 81

Gipsies, JOHN CLARE
  The snow falls deep; the forest lies alone
      COME 78   KEY II 102

The Gipsy Laddie, ANON

Black Jack Davy, ANON

The Wraggle-Taggle Gipsies, ANON
  It was late in the night when the squire came home
      FAB.C.V 173   OX.L.V 361   S.T.S I 2 (G)
  Black Jack Davy come a-ridin' through the woods
      PENG.A.F.S 192 (P,G)
  Three gipsies came to the castle gate
      BAL 539   B.P III 83   COME.79
      D.P.WAY 54   ECHO I 80   FIRE.F.S 70 (P)
      G.TR.P 96   KEY II 100   MER 246
      M.R.ON 69   OX.P.C 70   P.F.P I 51
      THIS.W.D 157

GNUS

G stands for Gnu, H. BELLOC
> G stands for Gnu, whose weapons of Defence
>> PEG IV 21

GOBLINS

Goblin Market (Part), CHRISTINA ROSSETTI
> Morning and evening
>> P.F.P II 198   P.P.OVER 82

Overheard on a Saltmarsh, H. MUNRO
> Nymph, nymph, what are your beads?
>> COME 124   PEG I 94   P.F.P I 110
>> THIS.W.D 33

GOLDFINCHES

A Goldfinch, WALTER DE LA MARE
> This feather-soft creature
>> B.B.F 6   BL.J II 44   DE LA M.CH 42

Goldfinches, JOHN KEATS
> Sometimes goldfinches one by one will drop
>> TREE IV 72

The Hollow Wood, EDWARD THOMAS
> Out in the sun the goldfinch flits
>> P.F.P I 123

GOLF

Seaside Golf, JOHN BETJEMAN
> How straight it flew, how long it flew
>> ALB.I 23   BET.P 195   M.CENT 30

GOLIATH
See also **David**

Goliath, WALTER DE LA MARE
> Still as a mountain with dark pines and sun
>> DE LA M.P I 50   TW.N 20

GRACE, W. G.

W.G., E. C. BENTLEY
    Dr W. G.
        PEG IV 3

GRACES
See also **Prayers**

The Selkirk Grace, ROBERT BURNS
    Some hae meat, and canna eat
        PEG V 31

A Sixteenth Century Grace, ANON
    God bless our meat
        BL.J 1 62

GRANDFATHERS

My Grandpa, TED HUGHES
    The truth of the matter, the truth of the matter
        B.P IV 20   HU.MEET 17

GRASSHOPPERS

Grasshoppers, JOHN CLARE
    Grasshoppers go in many a thrumming spring
        B.B.F 119   IRON 1 68

GREECE
See also **Alexander the Great**

On the Army of Spartans who died at Thermopylae, SIMONIDES OF CEOS
    Tell them in Lacedaemon, passer-by
        CHER 378

The Oracles, A. E. HOUSMAN
    'Tis mute, the word they went to hear
        on high Dodona mountain
        HOU.P 127

GYPSIES
See **Gipsies**

HANGING

HANNIBAL

Hannibal, ELEANOR FARJEON
>   Hannibal crossed the Alps!
>   P.LIFE II 43

HAPPINESS

The Enchanted Shirt, JOHN HAY
>   The king was sick; his cheek was red,
>   G.TR.P 171   M.R.FEEL 67   PEG I 5

HARDY, THOMAS

Afterwards, THOMAS HARDY
>   When the present has latched its postern
>   behind my tremulous stay
>   AN.E.P 165   AN.METH 106   AN.WAI 174
>   CHER 353   COME 455   HAR.PENG I 59
>   HAR.SEL 88   PEG V 88   P.TIME 71
>   P.TONG II 190   P.W 225

Thomas Hardy, WALTER DE LA MARE
>   Mingled the moonlight with daylight,
>   the last in narrowing west
>   DE LA M.CH 72

HARES

Epitaph on a Hare, WILLIAM COWPER
>   Here lies, whom hound did ne'er pursue
>   PENG.AN 138

The Hare, WALTER DE LA MARE
>   In the black furrow of a field
>   OX.V.J III 66

The Hunted Hare, ANON
>   By a forest as I 'gan fare
>   B.B.F 78

March Hares, ANDREW YOUNG
    I made myself as a tree
        YOU.P 47

HARVEST
See OX.V.J II 55
See also **Barley: Haymaking: Haystacks: Mowing**

HATE
Fire and Ice, ROBERT FROST
    Some say the world will end in fire
        FRO.P 268   FRO.PENG 141   FRO.YOU 82
        WEALTH 5

HAWKS
Hawk Roosting, TED HUGHES
    I sit in the top of the wood, my eyes closed
        EV.M 18   PENG.AN 140   PENG.NEW 153
        WHEEL IV 198
Hurt Hawks, ROBINSON JEFFERS
    The broken pillar of the wing jags from the clotted shoulder
        PENG.M.A.V 125
A Sparrow Hawk, ANON
    A Sparhawk did hold in wicked jail
        COME 108

HAYMAKING
Haymakers, EDWARD THOMAS
    Only the scent of woodbine and hay new-mown
        DRUM 66

HAYSTACKS
The Haystack, ANDREW YOUNG
    To dense to have a door
        DAWN 99   TREE III 94   YOU.P 200

HEAT

Satire on Paying Calls in August, CHINESE TRANS WALEY
   When I was young, throughout the hot season
      WAL.C.P 85

HEAVEN

General William Booth enters into Heaven, VACHEL LINDSAY
   Booth led boldly with his big bass drum
      FAB.M.V I58   LIN.P I23   SPIR 97

Heaven, RUPERT BROOKE
   Fish (fly-replete) in depth of June
      A.D.L I67   D.P.F.F 30   PAT 43
      P.P.BRA 65   P.TIME 62   WHEEL I I47

Heaven, EMILY DICKINSON
   Heaven is what I cannot reach
      KEY III 58

Jerusalem, my happy home, ANON
   Jerusalem, my happy home
      FAB.C.V 370

My Master hath a Garden, ANON
   My Master hath a garden, ful-filled with divers flowers
      B.P III I05   COME 492
   King Jesus hath a garden
      OX.S.M.S II 25 (M)

Peace, HENRY VAUGHAN
   My soul, there is a country
      CHER 347   D.P.F.F I8I   ECHO III 94
      EX.T.CH I85   FAB.C.V 368   OX.V.J III 85
      WEALTH 288

HEDGEHOGS

Hedgehog, ANTHONY THWAITE
   Twitching the leaves, just where the drainpipe clogs
      DAWN 64   HAP I7   UNDER 87

HENS

Clucking Hen, A. HAWKSHAWE
>   Pray will you take a walk with me
>>   EX.T.TRA 24   FAB.N.V 28   PUF.V 35

Hen and Carp, IAN SERRAILLIER
>   Once, in a roostery
>>   A.D.L 222   OX.V.J III 32   P.LIFE IV 11
>>   PUF.Q 157   TREE IV 24

HERMITS

Hermit and Politician, CHINESE TRANS WALEY
>   I was going to the city to sell the herbs I had plucked
>>   WAL.C.P 151

HEROD

Innocent's Song, CHARLES CAUSLEY
>   Who's that knocking on the window?
>>   DAWN 110
King Herod and the Cock, ANON
>   There was a star in David's land
>>   P.TONG 152

HERRING

Caller Herrin', LADY NAIRNE
>   Who'll buy my caller herrin'?
>>   OX.S.M.P 44 (M)

HIDE AND SEEK

Hide and Seek, VERNON SCANNELL
>   The sacks in the toolshed smell like the seaside
>>   HAP 29

HIGHWAYMEN
See also **Turpin, Dick**

Brennan on the Moor, ANON
    It's of a fearless highwayman a story now I'll tell
        BAL 745   FAB.BAL 204

The Wild Colonial Boy, ANON (Australian)
    'Tis of a wild colonial boy, Jack Doolan was his name
        FAB.BAL 229

HILLS
See **Mountains**

HIPPOPOTAMI

The Hippopotamus, H. BELLOC
    I shoot the hippopotamus
        BEL.PUF 102   ECHO III 50   MER 191
        PEG III 45   P.P.OVER 65   SPIR I

HIROSHIMA

Hiroshima, A SCHOOLCHILD
    Noon and hazy heat
        EV.M 77   WHEEL IV 210

No More Hiroshimas, JAMES KIRKUP
    At the station exit, my bundle in hand
        FLA 167

HISTORY
See also **England, History: Protests, Political: Rome: Scotland: Times Past: Trade Unions: U.S.A.: Vikings: War: Wars**

In the British Museum, THOMAS HARDY
    What do you see in that time-touched stone?
        HAR.PENG 118   HAR.SEL 63

Questions of a Studious Working Man, B. BRECHT
    Who built Thebes of the seven gates?
        MY 184

Verse, OLIVER ST. JOHN GOGARTY
    What should we know
        FAB.C.V 29   PEG II 100

HOBBYHORSES

The Centaur, MAY SWENSON
    The summer that I was ten—
        PENG.AN 60

HOBOES
See **Tramps**

HOLLY

The Holly, WALTER DE LA MARE
    The sturdiest of forest-trees
        P.SING 32

HOMES

Animals' Houses, JAMES REEVES
    Of animals' houses
        PUF.Q 75   REE. W. M 25

Cottage, ELEANOR FARJEON
    When I live in a cottage
        TREE I 13

Thanksgiving for his House, ROBERT HERRICK
    Lord, thou hast given me a cell
        CHER 269   OX.V.J IV 46   TREE III 32

HOMESICKNESS

Blows the wind today, R. L. STEVENSON
Blows the wind today, and the sun and the rain are flying
PEG II 14

Lament of Hsi-Chün, HSI-CHÜN TRANS WALEY
My people have married me
WAL.C.P 43

HORATIUS

Horatius, LORD MACAULAY
Lars Porsena of Clausium
FAB.C.V 150   P.P.FAL 75   SPIR 126

HORSES & PONIES
See also **Pegasus: Racing: Riding**

HORSES & PONIES (LYRIC & DESCRIPTIVE)

The Child in the Orchard, EDWARD THOMAS
He rolls in the orchard; he is stained with moss
THO.GR 35

The Horses, TED HUGHES
I climbed through the woods in the hour-before-dawn dark
ALB II 80   AN.JEN 130

Horses, EDWIN MUIR
Those lumbering horses in the steady plough
FLA 56

The Horses of the Sea, CHRISTINA ROSSETTI
The horses of the sea
BL.J I 55   OX.V.J II 79   TREE II 27

Horses on the Camargue, ROY CAMPBELL
In the grey wastes of dread
AN.SPO II 67   P.P.SAL 129   SCH.M.V 23

Jack and his Pony Tom, H. BELLOC
    Jack had a little pony, Tom
        FAB.N.V 173

The Stallion, WALT WHITMAN
    A gigantic beauty of a stallion,
        fresh and responsive to my caresses
        OX.V.J IV 39

Then the Lord answered Job, THE BIBLE
    Hast thou given the horse strength?
        BOOK OF JOB xxxix 19–25   PEG III 47
        P.W 84   TREE IV 19

HORSES & PONIES (NARRATIVE)

The Horses, EDWIN MUIR
    Barely a twelvemonth after
        R.R 185   THEME 154

How they brought the Good News from Ghent to Aix
    ROBERT BROWNING
    I sprang to the stirrup, and Joris, and he;
        G.TR.P 149   M.R.ON 14   PEG II 53
        P.REM 89   SPIR 29   WEALTH 146

Hunter Trials, JOHN BETJEMAN
    It's awf'lly bad luck on Diana
        ALB I 20   BET.P 236   DAWN 82
        V.F 23

The Man from Snowy River, A. B. PATERSON
    There was a movement at the station
        for the word had passed around
        WEALTH 148

Poor Old Horse, ANON
    My clothing was once of the linsey-wool fine
        COME 90   MER 216   M.R.HAND 60
        OX.S.M.S I 49 (M)

The Runaway, ROBERT FROST
>   Once when the snow of the year was beginning to fall

A.D.L 186	B.P III 37	COME 26
FAB.C.V 79	F.FEET 125	FRO.P 273
FRO.PENG 143	FRO.YOU 52	G.TR.P 29
HAP 68	KEY II 49	OX.V.J III 48

HOSTS
See **Guests**

HOUSEWIVES

The Housewife's Lament, ANON
>   One day I was walking, I heard a complaining
>   F.S.N.A 133 (G,B)   S.T.S I 56 (G)

On a Tired Housewife, ANON
>   Here lies a poor woman who was always tired

KEY III 58	MY 91	WEALTH 20

Robin-a-Thrush, ANON
>   O Robin-a-Thrush he married a wife!
>   TREE III 27

Washdays, ANON
>   They that wash on Monday
>   BL.J III 1

HUMAN RIGHTS
See also **Freedom Songs: Mankind: Refugees**

The Hammer Song, PETE SEEGER AND LEE HAYS
>   If I had a hammer
>   A.F.B 19 (G)   W.S.O 91 (G)

I am a Jew, WILLIAM SHAKESPEARE
>   I am a Jew
>   MERCHANT OF VENICE III i 56–71

A Man's a Man for a' that, ROBERT BURNS
    Is there for honest poverty
        OX.S.M.P 43 (M)

A New Hunting Song (c. 1846), ANON
    Now those that are low-spirited I hope won't think it wrong
        C.MUSE 137

The People of Tao-Chou, PO CHU-I TRANS WALEY
    In the land of Tao-Chou
        CHER 374

Prayer before Birth, LOUIS MACNEICE
    I am not yet born: oh hear me
        ALB II 112   AN.JEN 173   AN.WAI 184
        COM 91   DAY 23   PEG V 100
        PENG.C.V 195   WHEEL IV 174

A Song for the Spanish Anarchists, HERBERT READ
    The golden lemon is not made
        FLA 84

There lived a king, W. S. GILBERT
    There lived a king, as I've been told
        P.P.FAL 96

Thirty Bob a Week, JOHN DAVIDSON
    I couldn't touch a stop and turn a screw
        A.B.L.P 643

This land is your land, WOODY GUTHRIE
    As I went walking that ribbon of highway
        A.F.B 30 (G)

When wilt thou save the People? E. ELLIOTT
    When wilt thou save the People?
        WEALTH 290

HUMMING BIRDS
Humming-bird, D. H. LAWRENCE
    I can imagine, in some other world
        PENG.AN 150

HUNTING
See also **Foxes: Shooting**

A-hunting we will go, HENRY FIELDING
  The dusky night rides down the sky
     M.R.ON 65   TOM.T.G 77

Drink, Puppy, Drink, G. J. WHYTE-MELVILLE
  Here's to the fox in his earth below the rocks
     CH.GAR 60

The Hunt, WALTER DE LA MARE
  Tally-ho! Tally-ho!—
     DE LA M.CH 33

Hunting Song of the Seeonee Pack, RUDYARD KIPLING
  As the dawn was breaking the sambhur belled
     KIP.INC 648

John Peel, J. W. GRAVES
  D'ye ken John Peel with his coat so grey?
     D.P.JOU 102

The Keeper, ANON
  The Keeper did a-shooting go
     A.F.B 57 (G)   MER 118   OX.S.M.J II 26 (M)

The King's Hunt is Up, HENRY VIII (?)
  The hunt is up, the hunt is up
     B.P III 99   COME 137

Old Bangum, ANON
  There is a wild boar in these woods
     BAL 103

The Rabbit Hunter, ROBERT FROST
  Careless and still
     FRO.P 486   P.W 241

A Runnable Stag, J. DAVIDSON
  When the pods went pop on the broom, green broom
     KEY III 88   PENG.AN 295   P.F.P III 85

ICE
See **Frost & Ice: Skating: Winter**

ILLNESS
See also **Toothache**

The Sniffle, OGDEN NASH
    In spite of her sniffle
        WEALTH 25

INDIANS, RED

Hiawatha (Part), H. W. LONGFELLOW
    By the shore of Gitche Gumee
        WHEEL I 86
    Give me of your bark, O Birch-Tree
        SPIR 106   WHEEL I 92
    You shall hear how Pau Puk Keewis
        WHEEL II 94

Hiawatha (Part), H. W. LONGFELLOW
    Hiawatha's Childhood
        AP.SPO I 126   BL.J IV 25
    Hiawatha's Fishing
        AN.SPO I 127
    Hiawatha's Friends
        M.R.ON 33

Shenandoah, ANON
    O Shenandoah, I love your daughter
        A.F.B 17 (G)   B.L.A.F.S 138 (G,P)   FIRE.F.S 136 (P)
        F.S.N.A 53 (G,B)   IVES 134 (G,P)   PENG.A.F.S 40 (G,P)

INDUSTRY
See also **Factories: Machines: Trade Unions**

Fourpence a Day, ANON
    The ore's a-waiting in the tubs, the snow's upon the fell
        S.T.S I 51 (G)

INSECTS

See also **Ants: Bees: Beetles: Butterflies: Caterpillars: Centipedes: Crickets: Dragonflies: Flies: Gnats: Grasshoppers: Ladybirds: Mosquitoes: Moths: Scorpions: Spiders**

The Insect World, JOHN CLARE
>   The insect world amid the suns and dews
>   DRUM 71

The Temple of Nature (Part), ERASMUS DARWIN
>   The Wasp, fine architect, surrounds his domes
>   PENG.AN 154

INSIDE
See **Outside**

ISLANDS
See **Desert Islands**

ISRAEL

Song of a Hebrew, DANNIE ABSE
>   Working is another way of praying
>   JA.PO 10   MY 175

JACKDAWS

The Jackdaw of Rheims, R. H. BARHAM
>   The Jackdaw sat on the Cardinal's Chair
>   AN.SPO I 20   PENG.AN 160   P.F.P I 79

The Jackdaw on the Steeple, W. B. RANDS
>   There was a little jackdaw
>   TREE I 16

JACOB

The fox-coloured pheasant enjoyed his peace, P. LEVI
>   The fox-coloured pheasant enjoyed his peace
>   DAWN 36

JAGUARS

The Jaguar, TED HUGHES
  The apes yawn and adore their fleas in the sun
    GUN.HUG 43   THEME 49

JAMES I

James I (1603–25), RUDYARD KIPLING
  The child of Mary Queen of Scots
    KIP.INC 701

JAZZ (IMITATIVE)

And now, J. B. BOOTHROYD
  It's a rum—
    PEG IV 64

The Daniel Jazz, VACHEL LINDSAY
  Darius the Mede was a king and a wonder
    CHER 143   KEY IV 28   LIN.P I 59
    MY 59   P.F.P I 25   P.W 249
    WEALTH 168

Jazz Fantasia, CARL SANDBURG
  Drum on your drums, batter on your banjos
    WEALTH 257

JONAH

Jonah, T. BLACKBURN
  He stands in rags upon the heaving prow
    DAWN 38

JOSEPH

Joseph fell a-dreaming, ELEANOR FARJEON
  Joseph fell a-dreaming
    PUF.Q 20

JOSHUA

Joshua fit de Battle ob Jericho, ANON
Joshua fit de battle ob Jericho
A.F.B 37 (G)   FIRE.F.S 304 (P)

JOURNEYS

See also **Accidents: Aeroplanes: Exploring: Railways: Space Travel: Trains: Walking**

Ambition, MORRIS BISHOP
I got pocketed behind 7 X 3824
WHEEL IV 162

How many miles to Babylon? ANON
How many miles to Babylon?
FAB.C.V 284

Jog on, Jog on, WILLIAM SHAKESPEARE
Jog on, jog on the footpath way
WINTER'S TALE IV ii 133   FAB.C.V 295

John Gilpin, WILLIAM COWPER
John Gilpin was a citizen
A.B.L.P 350   CH.GAR 158   D.P.ROAD 119
P.P.FACT 55   V.F 39   WEALTH 101

The Naughty Boy, JOHN KEATS
There was a Naughty Boy
A.D.L 200   B.P.I 19   FAB.C.V 284
MER 204   OX.V.J I 32   P.LIFE III 37
P.P.OVER 14   PUF.V 122

The Railway Junction, WALTER DE LA MARE
From here through tunnelled gloom the track
DE LA M.CH 46

The Road not Taken, ROBERT FROST
Two roads diverged in a yellow wood
CHER 314   FAB.C.V 292   FRO.P 131
FRO.PENG 78   FRO.YOU 90   PAT 116
P.REM 197   SCH.M.V 54

The Rolling English Road, G. K. CHESTERTON
Before the Roman came to Rye or out to Severn strode
> CHES.P 203   D.P.F.F 79   FAB.C.V 292
> P.P.WIDE 9

KANGAROOS

The Kangaroo, ANON
Old Jumpety-Bumpety-Hop-and-Go-One
> TREE I 25

KEATS, JOHN

At Lulworth Cove a century back, THOMAS HARDY
Had I but lived a hundred years ago
> FLA 24   HAR.PENG 169

KIDD, CAPTAIN

Captain Kidd, ANON
My name was Robert Kidd
> F.S.N.A 15 (G)

Captain Kidd, R. AND S. VINCENT BENÉT
This person in the gaudy clothes
> P.LIFE III 11

KINGS & QUEENS
See also **England, History**
See also **Alexander the Great: Charles I: Charles II: David: Elizabeth I: Herod: James I: Nefertiti: Victoria**

Kings, WALTER DE LA MARE
King Canute
> PEG II 1   TREE II 41

The Kings of England, ANON
First William the Norman
> OX.N.R 113

KNIFE GRINDERS

The Knife Grinder, WALT WHITMAN
     Where the city's ceaseless crowd moves on the livelong day
         PEG V 15

KNIGHTS & LADIES (LYRIC & DESCRIPTIVE)

All in green my love went riding, E. E. CUMMINGS
     All in green my love went riding
         THIS.W.D 149

The Knight in prison, WILLIAM MORRIS
     Wearily, drearily
         P.REM 96

KNIGHTS & LADIES (NARRATIVE)

Eldorado, EDGAR ALLAN POE
     Gaily bedight
         BL.J III 9   PEG II 25

The Falcon, ANON
     Lully, lulley! Lully, lulley!
         BAL 692   COME 491   FAB.BAL 38
         MY 28

The Lady of Shalott, LORD TENNYSON
     On either side the river lie
         A.B.L.P 554   B.P IV 76   D.P.F.F 166
         PEG II 110   P.F.P II 184   P.P.FAL 29
         SPIR 138   WEALTH 139

Sir Eglamore, SAMUEL ROWLANDS
     Sir Eglamore that worthy knight
         MER 324   M.R.FEEL 77   P.REM 22

KOOKABURRAS

Kookaburra, ANON
     Kookaburra sits on an old gum-tree
         C.S.B 136 (P)

KRAKEN
The Kraken, LORD TENNYSON
    Below the thunders of the upper deep

| B.B.F 186 | KEY III 118 | PEG II 31 |
| PENG.AN 176 | P.LIFE IV 59 | THIS.W.D 119 |

LADYBIRDS
Cock-a-clay, JOHN CLARE
    In the cowslip pips I lay

| MER 258 | TREE IV 58 |

LAMBS
A Child's Voice, ANDREW YOUNG
    On winter nights shepherd and I

YOU.P 28

The lamb, WILLIAM BLAKE
    Little lamb, who made thee?

B.B.F 231	BLA.P 56	BLA.PENG 28
B.P I 46	CH.GAR 49	COME 93
EX.T.TRA 29	FAB.C.V 352	G.TR.P 34
OX.V.J I 36	PENG.AN 179	P.F.P I 92
TREE IV 77	WHEEL I 63	

Lamb, HUMBERT WOLFE
    The old bellwether

OX.V.J III 31

The Lambs of Grasmere, CHRISTINA ROSSETTI
    The upland flocks grew starved and thinned

| KEY II 56 | OX.V.J IV 44 |

On the Grassy Banks, CHRISTINA ROSSETTI
    On the grassy banks

TREE I 25

LAMENTS
See **Dirges & Laments**

LANDSCAPES

Fenland, ANDREW YOUNG
    Where sky is all around
        YOU.P 92

Passing T'ien-Mên Street in Ch'ang-an and seeing a Distant View of Chung-nan Mountains, CHINESE TRANS WALEY
    The snow has gone from Chung-nan; spring is almost come
        WAL.C.P 125

Teleg Song, CHINESE TRANS WALEY
    Teleg River
        WAL.C.P 113

LARKS

Hark! hark! the lark, WILLIAM SHAKESPEARE
    Hark! hark! the lark at heaven's gate sings
        CYMBELINE II iii 22   A.A 50   B.B.F 44
        CHER 264   OX.V.J II 18

The Lark in the Morning, ANON
    As I was a-walking
        CHER 41

The Lark's Nest, JOHN CLARE
    From yon black clump of wheat that grows
        BL.J III 55   KEY III 111

LAUGHING

Laughing Song, WILLIAM BLAKE
    When the green woods laugh with the voice of joy
        B.P III 88   CH.GAR 183   COME 198
        D.P.JOU 22   EX.T.TRO 73   F.Y.D 24
        OX.V.J I 35   P.W 139   THIS.W.D 91

Mrs. Reece Laughs, M. ARMSTRONG
    Laughter, with us, is no great undertaking
        PEG II 96   P.TIME 147   SCH.M.V 4
        V.F 17

LAZARUS
See **Dives & Lazarus**

LAZINESS

Lazy Man's Song, CHINESE TRANS WALEY
 I could have a job but am too lazy to choose it
   HAP 72   WAL.C.P 139

Pooh! WALTER DE LA MARE
 Dainty Miss Apathy
   DE LA M.CH 62

The Sluggard, ISAAC WATTS
 'Tis the voice of the sluggard, I heard him complain
   (parody by Carroll, KEY II 44)
   KEY II 43

LEAR, EDWARD

Edward Lear, EDWARD LEAR
 How pleasant to know Mr. Lear
   CHER 463   FAB.C.V 124   G.TR.P 212
   LEA.NON 7   OX.L.V 413   P.LIFE III 30
   P.P.OVER 23   V.F 100

LEPANTO

Lepanto, G. K. CHESTERTON
 White founts falling in the Courts of the sun
   A.D.L 245   AN.METH 37   AN.SPO II 16
   CHES.P 114   MOD 66   P.F.P II 12
   P.TIME 54   TW.N 22

LEVIATHAN

Leviathan, THE BIBLE
 Canst thou draw out Leviathan with a hook?
   BOOK OF JOB xli 1–34   AN.SPO I 80
   B.B.F 187   KEY IV 115

LIBRARY
See **Public Library**

LIGHTNING
See **Thunder & Lightning**

LIMERICKS

See BL.J II 56
FAB.N.V 218–24
KEY I 100

M.R.ON 39
OX.L.V 420, 488, 509
PEG I 15, 17, 23, 25

PENG.M.C 100, 286–7
P.LIFE IV 89
PUF.V 168
TREE III 42

CHER 27, 28, 31
G.TR.P 240–2
M.M.A 31, 44, 73, 78, 98, 102, 103
MY 91, 164, 165
OX.V.J II 96
PENG.COM 26, 79, 206, 234, 256
P.LIFE III 31, 47
P.P.OVER 56
TREE II 15
V.F 99, 175

LINCOLN, ABRAHAM

Abraham Lincoln walks at Midnight, VACHEL LINDSAY
    It is portentous and a thing of state
        LIN.P 53   SCH.M.V 94   SPIR 96
The Gettysburg Address (1863), ABRAHAM LINCOLN
    Fourscore and seven years ago our fathers brought
        forth on this continent a new nation
        AN.SPO II 52
Nancy Hanks, ROSEMARY BENÉT
    If Nancy Hanks
        SPIR 33

LINNETS

The Linnet, WALTER DE LA MARE
    Upon this leafy bush
        B.B.F 2   DE LA M.P I 184   P.F.P I 122

LIONS

LLAMAS

LOBSTERS

Lobster Quadrille, LEWIS CARROLL
    Will you walk a little faster

B.B.F 197	CHER 29	D.P.WAY 45
EX.T.TRO 53	MER 353	PENG.M.C 151
P.LIFE II 26	P.P.FACT 18	P.REM 27
P.TONG 185	V.F 30	

LOGGERS

The Frozen Logger, ANON
    As I sat down one evening
        F.S.N.A 120 (G,B)

The Jam on Gerry's Rock, ANON
    Come all ye trueborn shanty-boys whoever that ye be
        BAL 771   FAB.BAL 240

A Legend of Paul Bunyan, A. S. BOURINOT
    He came
        OX.V.J IV 22

LONDON

April 1709, JONATHAN SWIFT
    Now hardly here and there a hackney coach
        KEY IV 46

The Bells of London, ANON
    The Bells of London all fell wrangling
        M.R.FEEL 62

The Fire of London, JOHN DRYDEN
    At length the crackling noise and dreadful blaze
        R.R 61

London Bells (Oranges and Lemons), ANON
    Gay go up and gay go down

B.P I 74	EX.T.TRA 14	MER 60
OX.L.V 259	OX.N.R 68	P.P.SAL 61
PUF.V 178	TREE I 46	

LONELINESS

LOVERS (HAPPY) (NARRATIVE)

The Bailiff's Daughter of Islington, ANON
    There was a youth, and a well-beloved youth
        FAB.BAL 67   G.TR.P 114   M.R.ON 74
        OX.L.V 92

Hynd Horn, ANON
    In Scotland there was a baby born
        BAL 97   BUN 229   MER 278

Mia Carlotta, THOMAS DALY
    Guiseppe da barber, ees greata for mash
        WEALTH 207

A Subaltern's Love-Song, JOHN BETJEMAN
    Miss J. Hunter-Dunn, Miss J. Hunter-Dunn
        BET.P 97   M.CENT 40   SCH.M.V 9

Sweet Polly Oliver, ANON
    As sweet Polly Oliver lay musing in bed
        OX.S.M.J II 34 (M)

LOVERS (UNHAPPY) (LYRIC & DESCRIPTIVE)

Black Monday Lovesong, A. S. J. TESSIMOND
    In love's dances, in love's dances
        THEME 110

Down by the Salley Gardens, W. B. YEATS
    Down by the salley gardens
        IRON I 9   OX.S.M.S II 17 (M)   P.TIME 16
        YEA.P 22

Love without Hope, ROBERT GRAVES
    Love without hope, as when the young birdcatcher
        CHER 71   GRA.PENG 27   IRON I 87

O do not love too long, W. B. YEATS
    Sweetheart do not love too long
        PEG V 59   YEA.P 93

LOVERS (UNHAPPY) (NARRATIVE)

LOVE SONGS

Black is the Colour, ANON
     Black, black, black is the colour of my true love's hair
        B.L.A.F.S 56 (G,P)

Ca' the yowes, ROBERT BURNS
     Ca' the yowes to the knowes
        PEG V 58

Down in the Valley, ANON
     Down in the valley, valley so low
        A.F.B 33 (G)   B.L.A.F.S 62 (G,P)   FIRE F.S 99 (P)
        F.S.N.A 289 (G,B)   IVES 186 (G,P)
        PENG.A.F.S 198 (G,P)   WHEEL III 131

I know where I'm going, ANON
     I know where I'm going
        COM 18   PEG IV 113

O Mistress Mine, WILLIAM SHAKESPEARE
     O mistress mine, where are you roaming?
        TWELFTH NIGHT II iii 39   PEG III 68

O my luve's like a red red rose, ROBERT BURNS
     O my luve's like a red red rose
        CHER 64   COM 16   FAB.C.V 335
        PEG IV 110   P.REM 148   P.W 143
        R.R 146   WEALTH 83

LOVE SONGS (HAPPY)

The first time ever I saw your face, EWAN MACCOLL
     The first time ever I saw your face
        WHEEL IV 191

It was a lover and his lass, WILLIAM SHAKESPEARE
     It was a lover and his lass
        AS YOU LIKE IT V iii 15   COME 199
        C.S.B 104 (P)   MER 194   OX.S.M.S II 26

My true love hath my heart, SIR PHILIP SIDNEY
    My true love hath my heart and I have his
        COME 352   PEG IV 110

LOVE SONGS (UNHAPPY)

Careless Love, ANON
    Love, O love, O careless love
        A.F.B 11 (G)   B.L.A.F.S 64 (G,P)   FIRE.F.S 46 (P)
        F.S.N.A 585 (G,B)   IVES 192 (G,P)
        PENG.A.F.S 228 (G,P)

Dink's Song, ANON
    If I had wings like Noah's dove
        A.F.B 88 (G)   B.L.A.F.S 66 (G,P)   OX.L.V 464

Greensleeves, ANON
    Alas my love you do me wrong
        C.MUSE 304   C.S.B 98 (P)   OX.S.M.J III 52 (M)

Johnny has gone for a soldier, ANON
    There I sit on Butternut Hill
        B.L.A.F.S. 117 (G,P) FIRE.F.S 69 (P)   IVES 98 (G,P)
        S.N.W 23 (G,P)
    O Johnny dear has gone away
        F.S.N.A 47 (G,B,P)

Old Smoky, ANON
    On top of old Smoky
        A.F.B 60 (G)   BAL 739   B.L.A.F.S 60 (G,P)
        FIRE.F.S 42 (P)   F.S.N.A 221 (G,B)   IRON II 109
        PENG.A.F.S 38 (G,P)   S.N.W 36 (G,P)

O Waly, Waly, ANON
    O waly, waly up the bank
    The water is wide, I cannot get over
        A.F.B 77 (G)   BAL 550   FAB.BAL 143
        IRON II 180   PEG V 61   P.P.WIDE 50

LULLABIES

All the Pretty Little Horses, ANON
Hushaby (OR Hush-you-bye)
    B.L.A.F.S 14 (G,P)   C.S.B 90 (P)   OX.L.V 435
    PENG.A.F.S 96 (G,P)

Black Sheep, ANON
Black sheep, black sheep
    F.S.N.A 503 (G,B)

The Coventry Carol, ANON
Lully, lullay, thou little tiny child
    ECHO I 50

A Cradle Song, THOMAS DEKKER
Golden slumbers kiss your eyes
    BL.J III 4   COME 281   ECHO I 24
    MER 270   MY 177   OX.V.J II 16
    THIS.W.D 89   TREE IV 15

Hush-a-ba, birdie, croon, croon, ANON
Hush-a-ba, birdie, croon, croon
    ECHO I 38

Hush, little Baby, ANON
Hush, little baby, don't say a word
    PENG.A.F.S 97 (G,P)

The Infant King, BASQUE CAROL
Sing lullaby
    OX.S.M.S I 17

Nurse's Song, ANON
Sleep, Baby, sleep
    G.TR.P 301   M.R.HAND 9   MY 186
    THIS.W.D 88

On a Quiet Conscience, CHARLES I
Close thine eyes, and sleep secure
    P.P.TALK 80

Sometimes I feel, ANON
Sometimes I feel like a motherless child
A.F.B 49   B.L.A.F.S 368 (G,P)

Still the dark forest, W. H. AUDEN
Still the dark forest, quiet the deep
EX.T.TRO 88   OX.V.J I 71

Sweet and Low, LORD TENNYSON
Sweet and low, sweet and low
DRUM 29   G.TR.P 300   M.R.CHA 49
MY 185   OX.V.J I 40   THIS.W.D 87
TREE II 49

You spotted snakes, WILLIAM SHAKESPEARE
You spotted snakes with double tongue
MIDSUMMER NIGHT'S DREAM II ii 9   B.B.F 165
B.P IV 94   CH.GAR 18   D.P.JOU 103
EX.T.CH 28   F.FEET I 57   G.TR.P 297
MER 367   MY 27   OX.V.J II 75
P.LIFE II 78   P.REM 40   P.SING 50
THIS.W.D 37   TREE II 32

LYCHEES

The Lychee, WANG I TRANS WALEY
Fruit white and lustrous as a pearl
PEG V 31

MACHINES

The Guillotine, WILFRID GIBSON
Obedient to the will of men
KEY III 108   OX.V.J IV 22

The Horses, EDWIN MUIR
Barely a twelvemonth after
R.R 185   THEME I 54

Let us be Men, D. H. LAWRENCE
> For God's sake, let us be Men
>> M.P.W 65   PEG III 50

McAndrew's Hymn, RUDYARD KIPLING
> Lord, thou hast made this world below
> the shadow of a dream
>> A.B.L.P 646   KIP.INC 120

The Pigeon, RICHARD CHURCH
> Throb, throb from the mixer
>> M.R.CHA 58   P.F.P II 108   WEALTH 276

Portrait of a Machine, LOUIS UNTERMEYER
> What nudity so beautiful as this
>> DAY 125   M.R.CHA 63   PEG III 50
>> P.SING 137   R.R 73

The Secret of the Machines, RUDYARD KIPLING
> We were taken from the orebed and the mine
>> KIP.INC 709   M.R.CHA 60   P.F.P II 107
>> P.SING 132   R.R 74

A Trial Run, ROBERT FROST
> I said to myself almost in prayer
>> FRO.P 402   FRO.PENG 196   WEALTH 261

MAGIC
See also **Charms & Spells: Fantasy: Mystery**

Tom o' Bedlam, ANON
> The moon's my constant mistress
>> ECHO II 63   FAB.C.V 186   P.P.WIDE 85

MAGICIANS

The Two Magicians, ANON
> O she looked out of the window
>> MER 341

The Witch Stepmother, ANON
    I was but seven year old
        MER 358

MALLARD

Mallard, REX WARNER
    Squawking they rise from reeds into the sun
        R.R 183   THEME 65

MAN IN THE MOON

The Man in the Moon, J. W. RILEY
    Said the Raggedy Man, on a hot afternoon
        PENG.YET 77

MANKIND
See also **Portraits**

anyone lived in a pretty how town, E. E. CUMMINGS
    anyone lived in a pretty how town
        CUM.PENG 44   PENG.M.A.V 184   WHEEL IV 163

Prayer before Birth, LOUIS MACNEICE
    I am not yet born: oh, hear me
        ALB II 112   AN.JEN 173   AN.WAI 84
        COM 91   DAY 23   PEG V 100
        PENG.C.V 195   WHEEL IV 174

The Unknown Citizen, W. H. AUDEN
    He was found by the Bureau of Statistics to be
        DAY 10   R.R 130   THEME 144

MARCH

Written in March, WILLIAM WORDSWORTH
    The cock is crowing
        BL.J II 32   B.P IV 71   G.TR.P 270
        KEY II 90   MER 362   M.R.FEEL 46
        P.SING 22   THIS.W.D 103   TOM.T.G 37

MARCHING

Boots (Infantry columns), RUDYARD KIPLING
　　　　We're foot—slog—slog—slog—slogging over Africa
　　　　KIP.INC 465

Marching Song, R. L. STEVENSON
　　　　Bring the comb and play upon it
　　　　M.R.FEEL 8

Roman Road, A. G. PRYS-JONES
　　　　This is the way the Romans came
　　　　AN.SPO I 142

Shadow March, R. L. STEVENSON
　　　　All round the house is the jet-black night
　　　　OX.V.J II 16　　　　P.LIFE III 94

The Song of Soldiers, WALTER DE LA MARE
　　　　As I sat musing by the frozen dyke
　　　　AN.E.P 162　　　　DE LA M.P II 242

We be the King's Men, THOMAS HARDY
　　　　We be the king's men hale and hearty
　　　　COME 175　　　　DRUM 15　　　　EX.T.CH 105
　　　　MER 346　　　　M.R.FEEL 27　　　　TOM.T.G 137

MARIGOLDS

How Marigolds came Yellow, ROBERT HERRICK
　　　　Jealous girls these sometimes were
　　　　CHER 268

MARRIAGE

An Arundel Tomb, PHILIP LARKIN
　　　　Side by side, their faces blurred
　　　　FLA 163

The Curate's Kindness: A Workhouse Irony, THOMAS HARDY
　　　　I thought there'd be strangers around me
　　　　HAR.PENG 68

The Dumb Wife Cured, ANON
    There was a bonny blade
        AN.SPO I 5

Father Grumble, ANON
    Father Grumble he did say
        BAL 747

The Forsaken Merman, MATTHEW ARNOLD
    Come dear children, let us away

AN.E.P 146	AN.SPO I 32	CH.GAR 34
DRUM 41	EX.T.CH 174	FAB.C.V 325
MY 68	OX.P.C 59	OX.V.J III 57
P.F.P II 214	P.P.BRA 51	P.W 210
SPIR 121		

Get up and Bar the Door, ANON
    It fell about the Martinmas time

AN.SPO I 8	BAL 657	FAB.BAL 77
G.TR.P 123	PEG I 90	P.F.P I 154
P.P.BRA 24		

mehitabel tries marriage, DON MARQUIS
    boss I have seen mehitabel the cat
        WEALTH 202

The Old Man in the Wood, ANON
    There was an old man who lived in a wood
        MER 129

MARTHA

Martha of Bethany, C. SANSOM
    It's all very well
        AN.SPO II 129   THEME 130

The Sons of Martha, RUDYARD KIPLING
    The sons of Mary seldom bother
        KIP.INC 377

MARTINS

Martins: September, WALTER DE LA MARE
 At secret daybreak they had met
  DE LA M.CH 50

MARTYRS

The Martyrdom of Bishop Farrar, TED HUGHES
 Bloody Mary's venomous flames can curl
  THEME 82

More light! More light! ANTHONY HECHT
 Composed in the Tower before his execution
  PENG.C.A.P 75

MAY

The May Magnificat, GERARD MANLEY HOPKINS
 May is Mary's month, and I
  OX.V.J IV 65

Merry May, PERCIVAL LEIGH
 The sky scowls
  KEY III 81   PENG.M.C 232

Now is the month of Maying, THOMAS MORLEY
 Now is the month of Maying
  C.S.B 112 (P)

An Unkindly May, THOMAS HARDY
 A shepherd stands by a gate in a white smock frock
  HAR.PENG 202

MAY DAY

Corinna's Going a Maying, ROBERT HERRICK
 Get up, get up for shame, the blooming morn
  A.D.L 35   P.P.WIDE 83   P.W 96

Home Pictures in May, JOHN CLARE
 The sunshine bathes in clouds of many hues
  KEY III 80

Maypole Dance (1671), ANON
    Come lasses and lads

        D.P JOU 94   OX.L.V 190   WEALTH 240

MEDICINE (HISTORIC)

Our Fathers of Old, RUDYARD KIPLING
    Excellent herbs had our fathers of old
        KIP.INC 548

MERMAIDS & MERMEN (LYRIC & DESCRIPTIVE)

Full fathom five, WILLIAM SHAKESPEARE
    Full fathom five thy father lies

TEMPEST I ii 394	AN.E.P 32	B.P II 53
CHER 231	COM 187	D.P.WAY 119
DRUM 39	ECHO I 24	FAB.C.V 268
KEY III 118	MER 270	MY 29
OX.V.J IV 89	PENG.E.V 67	P.F.P I 111
P.P.BRA 47	P.REM 202	P.W 65
THIS.W.D 83		

The Mermaid, LORD TENNYSON
    Who would be
        TREE IV 36

The Mermaids, WALTER DE LA MARE
    Sand, sand; hills of sand
        DE LA M.CH 86   DE LA M.P I 91   DRUM 42

MERMAIDS & MERMEN (NARRATIVE)

The Forsaken Merman, MATTHEW ARNOLD
    Come, dear children, let us away

AN.E.P 146	AN.SPO I 32	CH.GAR 34
DRUM 41	EX.T.CH 174	FAB.C.V 325
MY 68	OX.P.C 59	OX.V.J III 57
P.F.P II 214	P.P.BRA 51	P.W 210
SPIR 121		

Little Fan, JAMES REEVES
    'I don't like the look of little Fan, Mother'
        V.F 112

On a Friday morn, ANON
    On a Friday morn as we set sail
        BAL. 673   B.P III 72   COME 421
        EX.T.CH 26   P.F.P I 57   TOM.T.G 130

Sam, WALTER DE LA MARE
    When Sam goes back in memory
        DE LA M.P II 187   WEALTH 160

MICE

Anne and the Field-Mouse, IAN SERRAILLIER
    We found a mouse in the chalk quarry today
        SER.HAP 8

The Mouse, E. COATSWORTH
    I hear a mouse
        PUF.V 45

Mouse, DAVID SHAVREEN
    Mouse, mouse, who lives in our house
        TREE II 58

Supper, WALTER DE LA MARE
    Her pinched grey body
        DE LA M.CH 129

MINERS

The Avondale Mine Disaster, ANON
    Good Christians all, both great and small
        BAL 783

The Ballad of Springhill, EWAN MACCOLL
    In the town of Springhill, Nova Scotia
        WHEEL II 165

Miners, WILFRED OWEN
>There was a whispering on my hearth
>>ECHO III 134

The Pit, WILFRID GIBSON
>With twinkling watery eyes and wheezily
>>WHEEL III 142

MINNOWS

The Minnow, E. L. M. KING
>Of all the fishes great and small
>>TREE I 66

MIRRORS

The Magical Picture, ROBERT GRAVES
>Glinting on the Roadway
>>GRA.FID 48

MNEMONICS

Four Dates, ANON
>William the Conquerer, ten sixty-six
>>BL.J II 2

Kings of England, ANON
>First William the Norman
>>OX.N.R I 13

The Signs of the Zodiac, ANON
>The Ram, the Bull, the Heavenly Twins
>>Y.B.S ix

MOLE CATCHERS

The Molecatcher, ANON
>A molecatcher I and that is my trade
>>OX.S.M.P 48 (M)

Mole Catcher, EDMUND BLUNDEN
>With coat like any mole's, as soft and black
>>R.R 127

MOLES

A Dead Mole, ANDREW YOUNG
  Strong-shouldered mole
    PENG.AN 203   YOU.P 174

MONEY

The Hardship of Accounting, ROBERT FROST
  Never ask of money spent
    FAB.C.V 374   FRO.P 408   FRO.PENG 199

MONKEYS
See **Apes & Monkeys**

MONSTERS
See also **Animals, Fantastic: Dragons: Giants: Ogres: Sea Monsters: Trolls**

Behemoth and Leviathan, THE BIBLE
  Behold now Behemoth which I made with thee
    BOOK OF JOB xl and xli   KEY IV 114

The Dinotherium, H. BELLOC
  The dreadful Dinotherium, he
    KEY IV 147

The Wendigo, OGDEN NASH
  The Wendigo
    FAB.N.V 80   KEY IV 59   NA.P.D.R 70

MONTHS
See also **April: August: March: May: November: October**

The Months, ANON
  Januar: By thys fyre I warme my handys
    CHER 425

Months of the Year, SARA COLERIDGE
  January brings the snow
    B.P II 59   G.TR.P 268   P.LIFE I 54
    PUF.V 15   TOM.T.G 35   TREE III 20

MOODS
See **Anger: Happiness: Hate: Introspection: Laughing: Laziness: Loneliness: Obstinacy**

MOON
See also **Man in the Moon**

Above the Dock, T. E. HULME
    Above the quiet dock in midnight
        BL.J II 50   P.W 252   WEALTH 270

Autumn, T. E. HULME
    A touch of cold in the autumn night
        FLA 40   MY 10   P.W 252

Full Moon, WALTER DE LA MARE
    One night as Dick lay half asleep
        DE LA M.P. II 188

Is the moon tired? CHRISTINA ROSSETTI
    Is the moon tired? She looks so pale
        MER 193   M.R.ON 64

The Moon, R. L. STEVENSON
    The moon has a face like the clock in the hall
        TREE II 30

The Moon, EMILY DICKINSON
    The moon was but a chin of gold
        OX.V.J I 40

The Moon's the North Wind's Cooky, VACHEL LINDSAY
    The moon's the north wind's cooky
        G.TR.P 258   LIN.P 67

Riddle on Moon and Sun, ANGLO-SAXON TRANS BONE
    I saw a creature sally with booty
        P.W 31

Silver, WALTER DE LA MARE
    Slowly, silently, now the moon
        AN.METH 56   DE LA M.P II 232   G.TR.P 262
        KEY III 138   MER 323   OX.V.J III 71
        P.F.P I 37   P.LIFE III 90   P.P.FACT 52
        P.SING 37

Welcome to the Moon, ANON
    Welcome, precious stone of the night
        CHER 403

What the Snowman said, VACHEL LINDSAY
    The moon's a snowball. See the drifts
      LIN.P 241

MOSES

Go Down, Moses, ANON
    When Israel was in Egypt's land
        B.L.A.F.S 372 (G,P)   FIRE.F.S 316 (P)   PENG.A.F.S 138 (G,P)

MOSQUITOES

Mosquito, D. H. LAWRENCE
    When did you start your tricks
        PENG.AN 210   PENG.C.V 77

MOTHERS

Daughters and Mothers, WALTER DE LA MARE
    Oh yes my dear, you have a mother
        JOY 145

To my Mother, GEORGE BARKER
    Most near, most dear, most loved and most far
        FAB.M.V 332   M.P.W 4   PENG.C.V 263

MOTHS

The Moth, WALTER DE LA MARE
    Isled in the midnight air
        DE LA M.CH 56

Psalm 121, THE BIBLE
>I will lift up mine eyes unto the hills
>>DRUM 43

MOWING

Mowing, ROBERT FROST
>There was never a sound beside the wood but one
>>FRO.P 25   FRO.PENG 24

The Scythe, S. SNAITH
>This morning as the scythe swings in my grasp
>>PEG V 36

MULES

Mule, ANON
>My mammy was a wall-eyed goat
>>PENG.M.C 267

MURDER

The Dorking Thigh, W. PLOMER
>About to marry and invest
>>WEALTH 198

Edward, Edward, ANON
>Why does your brand sae drop wi' blude?
>>AN.SPO II 9   BAL 86   BUN 39
>>COM 108   COME 430   FAB.BAL II9
>>IRON I 72   KEY I 19   PEG III 89
>>P.F.P I 149   P.P.TALK 72   P.W 4
>>WHEEL III 25
>What makes that blood on the point of your knife?
>>ECHO II 49   IVES 48 (G,P)
>What bluid's that on thy coat lap?
>>BAL 85

Lord Randal, ANON
>Oh where hae ye been, Lord Randal my son?
>>BAL 81 FAB.BAL 34 IVES 58 (G,P)
>>M.R.HAND 72 OX.V.J IV 22 P.F.P I 147
>>P.P.TALK 74 P.TONG 101 P.W. 16
>>R.R 26

The Murder of Maria Marten, W. CORDER
>Come all you thoughtless young men, a warning take by me
>>C.MUSE 270

The Other Time, PETER APPLETON
>He killed a man
>>KEY IV 18

The Two Brothers, ANON
>There were two brethren in the North
>>PEG II 67

Young Molly Ban, ANON (Irish)
>Come all you young fellows that follow the gun
>>BAL 700 FAB.BAL 206

MUSHROOMS

Mushrooms, SYLVIA PLATH
>Overnight, very
>>THEME 55

MUSIC

See also **Bagpipes: Bands: Banjos: Bugles: Fiddles, see Violins: Jazz, Imitative: Lullabies: Pipers: Singing: Spirituals: Violins**

Be not afeard, WILLIAM SHAKESPEARE
>Be not afeard, the isle is full of noises
>>TEMPEST III ii 141 P.W 75

How sweet the moonlight sleeps upon this bank, WILLIAM SHAKESPEARE
>How sweet the moonlight sleeps upon this bank
>>MERCHANT OF VENICE V i 54 P.W 74

Laudate Dominum, THE BIBLE
    O praise God in his holiness
        PSALM 150   CHER 446

Orpheus with his Lute, WILLIAM SHAKESPEARE (?)
    Orpheus with his lute made trees
        HENRY VIII III i 3   AN.SPO I 150   D.P.F.F 127
        FAB.N.V 36   M.R.CHA 46   P.SING 141

Piano, D. H. LAWRENCE
    Softly, in the dusk, a woman is singing to me
        R.R 112

Song for St. Cecilia's Day, JOHN DRYDEN
    From harmony, from heavenly harmony
        AN.SPO II 82   P.W 116
    an extract:
        PEG IV 61

MYSTERY (LYRIC & DESCRIPTIVE)
See also **Fantasy**

'O where are you going?' said reader to rider, W. H. AUDEN
    'O where are you going?' said reader to rider
        AN.E.P 177   AUD.PENG 24   FAB.C.V 294
        WHEEL IV 180

Song of the Mad Prince, WALTER DE LA MARE
    Who said 'Peacock pie'?
        DE LA M.CH 127   DE LA M.P II 249   FAB.C.V 282
        IRON II 129   MY 32   P.P.OVER 62
        P.TONG 184   R.R 115

Tom o' Bedlam, ANON
    The moon's my constant mistress
        ECHO II 63   FAB.C.V 186   P.P.WIDE 85

Warning to Children, ROBERT GRAVES
    Children, if you dare to think
        DAY 40   FAB.C.V 98   GRA.FID 62
        GRA.P 46   GRA.PENG 47   PENG.C.V 128

The Way through the Woods, RUDYARD KIPLING
    They shut the road through the woods

COME 297	D.P.F.F 64	FAB.C.V 377
KIP.INC 482	OX.V.J IV 63	P.F.P II 223
P.LIFE IV 26	P.P.FAL 53	P.SING 76
P.TIME 37	THIS.W.D 163	WEALTH 218

When I set out for Lyonesse, THOMAS HARDY
    When I set out for Lyonesse
        HAR.PENG 89

Which? WALTER DE LA MARE
    What did you say?
        DE LA M.CH 100

MYSTERY (NARRATIVE)

Flannan Isle, W. W. GIBSON
    Though three men dwell on Flannan Isle

AN.METH 84	COME 415	M.M.A 11
M.R.ON 89	OX.P.C 78	P.F.P II 219
R.R 29	TW.N 116	WEALTH 162

Goblin Market, CHRISTINA ROSSETTI
    Morning and evening
        P.F.P II 198   P.P.OVER 82

The Listeners, WALTER DE LA MARE
    'Is there anybody there?' said the Traveller

AN.METH 57	B.P IV 67	DE LA M.CH 99
DE LA M.P I 162	D.P.F.F 70	P.LIFE IV 42
P.P.FAL 12	P.SING 75	P.TIME 26
THIS.W.D 147	TW.N 120	WHEEL III 141

Lollocks, ROBERT GRAVES
    By sloth in sorrow fathered

CHER 155	DAY 38	GRA.P 190
GRA.PENG 140	KEY IV 60	PENG.C.V 132

Someone, WALTER DE LA MARE
    Someone came knocking
        DE LA M.P II 119   EX.T.H 33   OX.V.J I 43
        PUF.V 187

A Strange Meeting, W. H. DAVIES
    The moon is full, and so am I
        M.R CHA 31   OX.P.C 148   P.REM 114

Welsh Incident, ROBERT GRAVES
    But that was nothing to what things came out
        ALB I 71   COM 121   GRA.P 108
        GRA.PENG 86   PEG IV 22   PENG.C.V 129
        P.F.P II 222   R.R. 178   WEALTH 196

MYTHOLOGY
See **Balder: Cyclops: Orpheus: Pan: Pegasus: Shiv**

NAAMAN

Naaman, NORMAN NICHOLSON
    So this is the river ! Cold and still as steel
        M.CENT 93

NAMES

American Names, S. V. BENÉT
    I have fallen in love with American names
        PEG V 66   PENG.M.A.V 194

Boys' and Girls' Names, ELEANOR FARJEON
    What splendid names for boys there are !
        P. LIFE II 9

Choosing their Names, THOMAS HOOD
    Our old cat has kittens three
        TREE III 56

Etude Géographique, STODDARD KING
    Out west, they say, a man's a man; the legend still persists
        P.P.OVER 80

Jargon, JAMES REEVES
    Jerusalem, Joppa, Jericho—
        HAP 51   V.F 116

Names for Twins, ALASTAIR REED
    Each pair of twins
        TREE III 58

The Naming of Cats, T. S. ELIOT
    The Naming of Cats is a difficult matter
        ALB I 63   CH.GAR 54   EL.O.P 11

Two Men, E. ARLINGTON ROBINSON
    There be two men of all mankind
        G.TR.P 91

NAPOLEON

Boney was a Warrior, ANON
    Boney was a Warrior
        OX.S.M.J I 42 (M)   P.W 25

Napoleon, WALTER DE LA MARE
    What is the world, O soldiers?
        DE LA M.CH 139   DE LA M.P I 35   FAB.C.V 147
        P.REM 117

St. Helena Lullaby, RUDYARD KIPLING
    How far is St. Helena from a little child at play?
        FAB.C.V 147   KIP INC 517   P.P.BRA 71
        P.TIME 68   SCH.M.V 80

We be the King's Men, THOMAS HARDY
    We be the King's men, hale and hearty
        COME 175   DRUM 15   EX.T.CH.105
        MER 346   M.R.FEEL 27   TOM.T.G 137

NAVY
See **Sailors: Slave Trade**

NEFERTITI

Queen Nefertiti, ANON
> Spin a coin, spin a coin
>> MY 22

NEIGHBOURS

Mending Wall, ROBERT FROST
> Something there is that doesn't love a wall
>> ECHO II 54   FRO.P 47   FRO.PENG 32
>> FRO.YOU 70   IRON II 44   M.P.W 37

NELSON
See also **Trafalgar**

The Death of Nelson, ANON
> Come all gallant seamen that unite a meeting
>> C.MUSE 132   OX.L.V 402

1805, ROBERT GRAVES
> At Viscount Nelson's lavish funeral
>> DAY 35   FAB.C.V 146   GRA.P 219
>> GRA.PENG 161   P.F.P II 73   P.W 264
>> R.R 51

NETTLES

Tall Nettles, EDWARD THOMAS
> Tall nettles cover up, as they have done
>> CHER 237   IRON I 38   PAT 167
>> P.TIME 87   THO.GR 30   THO.SEL 35
>> TREE IV 95

G

NEW YEAR

A New Year Carol, ANON
>   Here we bring new water
>> COME 4   ECHO III 37   MER 300
>> OX.V.J II 86   P.P.WIDE 12   THIS.W.D 96
>> TOM.T.G 115

Wassail Song, ANON
>   Here we come awassailing among the leaves so green
>> C.S.B 130 (P)   OX.S.M.P 18 (M)

NIGHT

Acquainted with the Night, ROBERT FROST
>   I have been one acquainted with the night
>> CHER 402   FRO.P 324   FRO.PENG 161
>> FRO.YOU 25

Check, JAMES STEPHENS
>   Night was creeping on the ground!
>> AN.SPO I 152   OX.V.J I 41

The Country Bedroom, FRANCES CORNFORD
>   My room's a square and candle-lighted boat
>> OX.V.J III 55

Midnight, THOMAS SACKVILLE
>   Midnight was come, when every living thing
>> TREE IV 47

Midnight's Bell, THOMAS MIDDLETON
>   Midnight's bell goes ting, ting, ting
>> B.B.F 104   OX.V.J I 27

The Moon has set, SAPPHO
>   The Moon has set
>> CHER 404

Out in the Dark, EDWARD THOMAS
>   Out in the dark over the snow
>> COME 474   DRUM 35   ECHO II 48
>> P.P.FAL 108   THO.GR 74   THO.SEL 24

NOISE
See also **Sounds**

NONSENSE

Adventures of Isabel, OGDEN NASH
    Isabel met an enormous bear

        A.D.L 241   EX.T.CH 78   FAB.N.V 105
        OX.V.J IV 73   P.LIFE II 11

Alas, Alack! WALTER DE LA MARE
    Ann, Ann!

        DE LA M.P. II 111   FAB.N.V 64   MER 88
        PEG I 99   TREE I 59

Brian O Linn, ANON (Irish)
    Brian O Linn had no breeches to wear

        FAB.BAL 199   V.F 168

The Common Cormorant, ANON
    The common cormorant or shag

        A.D.L 227   G.TR.P 223   MY 158
        PENG.COM 240   P.P.WIDE 41   P.TONG 123
        SPIR I

Eletelephony, L. RICHARDS
    Once there was an elephant

        FAB.N.V 56   P.LIFE III 87

Fire, Fire! ANON
    Fire, Fire said Mrs. McGuire

        P.LIFE I 16   PUF.N.R 174–5

The Month of Liverpool, ANON
    'Twas in the month of Liverpool

        TREE I 44

My Chair, ANON
    As I was sitting in my chair

        TREE I 61

Poor Old Woman, ANON
    There was an old woman who swallowed a fly

        BL.J III 10   KEY I 13   PEG I 24

NONSENSE (CARROLL)

Father William, LEWIS CARROLL
　　'You are old, Father William' the young man said

ECHO I 99	G.TR.P 206	PENG.COM 259
P.P.BRA 79	TREE III 86	V.F 28

The Hunting of the Snark (Part), LEWIS CARROLL
　　Just the place for a Snark

M.M.A 107	PENG.M.C 103

　　There was one who was famed for the number of things

M.R.ON 41

Jabberwocky, LEWIS CARROLL
　　'Twas brillig, and the slithy toves

A.D.L 221	AN.SPO I 103	B.P IV 70
G.TR.P 208	MER 283	M.M.A 91
PEG I 34	PENG.M.C 184	P.P.TALK 10
P.W 216	SPIR 4	WHEEL II 122

Lobster Quadrille, LEWIS CARROLL
　　Will you walk a little faster

B.B.F 197	CHER 29	D.P.WAY 45
EX.T.TRO 53	MER 353	PENG.M.C 151
P.LIFE II 26	P.P.FACT 18	P.REM 27
P.TONG 185	V.F 30	

The Mad Gardener's Song, LEWIS CARROLL
　　He thought he saw an Elephant

AN.SPO I 25	B.P IV 91	D.P.WAY 39
EX.T.CH 82	FAB.N.V 144	M.M.A 75
PEG I 14	PENG.COM 232	P.P.TALK 34
PUF.V 169	SPIR 5	TREE IV 14
WHEEL I 116		

The Walrus and the Carpenter, LEWIS CARROLL
　　The sun was shining on the sea

PENG.M.C 147	P.P.TALK 66	P.REM 108
TOM.T.G 95	TREE IV 52	

The Owl and the Pussycat, EDWARD LEAR
    The Owl and the Pussycat went to sea

The Pelican Chorus, EDWARD LEAR
    King and Queen of the Pelicans we

The Pobble who has no Toes, EDWARD LEAR
    The Pobble who has no toes

NOVEMBER
See also **Guy Fawkes Night**

November, R. W. DIXON
    The feather of the willow

November, TED HUGHES
    The month of the drowned clog. After long rain the land

November, E. THOMAS
    November's days are thirty

November, JOHN CLARE
    The shepherds almost wonder where they dwell

November in London, THOMAS HOOD
      No sun—no moon!
   CHER 392   G.TR.P 280   OX.P.C 99
   PEG I 106   P.REM 113   R.R 89

November Night, A. CRAPSEY
      Listen . . .
   WEALTH 225

November Skies, JOHN FREEMAN
      Than these November skies
   AN.SPO II 86

NUCLEAR WAR
See also **Hiroshima**

It is almost the year two thousand, ROBERT FROST
      To start the world of old
   FRO.P 488   FRO.PENG 234   PEG V 115

The Responsibility, PETER APPLETON
      I am the man who gives the word
   R.R 58

Your Attention Please, PETER PORTER
      The Polar DEW has just warned that
   FLA 191   HERE 120   THEME I 52
   UNDER I 10

NUMBERS
Roman Figures, ANON
      X shall stand for playmates ten
   BL.J II 23

NYMPHS
Overheard on a saltmarsh, HAROLD MUNRO
      Nymph, nymph, what are your beads?
   COME 124   PEG I 94   P.F.P I 110
   THIS.W.D 33

OAKS

The Beech and the Sapling Oak, T. L. PEACOCK
> For the tender beech and the sapling oak
>> KEY IV 23

The Hill Pines, ROBERT BRIDGES
> The hill pines were sighing
>> KEY IV 23

OBSTINACY

Get up and Bar the Door, ANON
> It fell about the Martinmas time

AN.SPO I 8	BAL 657	FAB.BAL 77
G.TR.P 123	PEG I 90	P.F.P I 154
P.P.BRA 24		

OCCASIONS

See **Christmas: Easter: Epiphany: Guy Fawkes Night: May
Day: New Year**

OCCUPATIONS

See **Trades & Professions**

OCTOBER

October's Song, ELEANOR FARJEON
> The forest's afire!
>> A.D.L 99

Poem in October, DYLAN THOMAS
> It was my thirtieth year to heaven

DAWN 102	M.CENT 158	PEG V 32
WEALTH 231		

OCTOPI

The Octopus, OGDEN NASH
> Tell me, O Octopus, I begs

KEY II 84	NA.P.B 161	PENG.YET 84
WEALTH 24		

OGRES

The Ogre, WALTER DE LA MARE
'Tis moonlight on Trebarwith sands
DE LA M.CH 82

OLD AGE

His Golden Locks, G. PEELE
His golden locks Time hath to silver turned
P.W 57   R.R 102

I look into my Glass, THOMAS HARDY
I look into my glass
THEME 101

Old Dan'l, L. A. G. STRONG
Out of his cottage to the sun
M.R.CHA 29

The Song of the Mother, W. B. YEATS
I rise in the dawn and I kneel and I blow
PEG V 101   TREE IV 33

OPTIMISTS

Lucy Lake, OGDEN NASH
Lawsamassy, for heaven's sake!
NA.P.B 96

The Optimist, D. H. LAWRENCE
The optimist builds himself safe inside a cell
M.P.W 65

ORPHANS

The Orphan, CHINESE TRANS WALEY
To be an orphan
WAL.C.P 49

ORPHEUS

Orpheus with his Lute, WILLIAM SHAKESPEARE (?)
    Orpheus with his lute made trees

        HENRY VIII III i 3   AN.SPO I 150   D.P.F.F 127
        FAB.N.V 36   M.R.CHA 46   P.SING 141

OTTERS

An Otter, TED HUGHES
    Underwater eyes, an eel's

        COM 51   DAWN 66   GUN.HUG 57
        PENG.AN 227   PENG.C.V 381   PENG.NEW 158

OUTLAWS

Jesse James, W. R. BENÉT
    Jesse James was a two-gun man

        PEG I 74   SPIR 167

OUTSIDE & INSIDE

The Fallow Deer at the Lonely House, THOMAS HARDY
    One without looks in tonight

        B.B.F 113   HAR.SEL 24   OX.V.J III 62
        TREE IV 82

OWLS

The Barn Owl, SAMUEL BUTLER
    White moonlight, silvering all the walls

        MY 122

My Grandpa, TED HUGHES
    The truth of the matter, the truth of the matter

        B.P IV 20   HU.MEET 17

The Owl, EDWARD THOMAS
    Downhill I came, hungry, and yet not starved

        FLA 38   THO.SEL 27

The Owl, WALTER DE LA MARE
    Owl of the wildwood

        ALB I 56   HAP 50

The Ox Tamer, WALT WHITMAN
      In a faraway northern county in the placid pastoral region
            KEY IV 150
Twelve Oxen, ANON
      I have twelve oxen that be fair and brown
            DRUM 49   ECHO I 39

OYSTERS

The Exeter Book (Part), ANON TRANS K. G. HOLLAND
      The deep sea suckled me, the waves sounded over me
            PENG.AN 229
The Walrus and the Carpenter, LEWIS CARROLL
      The sun was shining on the sea
            PENG.M.C 147   P.P.TALK 66   P.REM 108
            TOM.T.G 95   TREE IV 52

PAINTERS
See **Chardin**

PAINTING (POEMS FOR PICTURE-MAKING)
See PRE.AN throughout
All in green my love went riding, E. E. CUMMINGS
      All in green my love went riding
            THIS.W.D 149
The Ancient Mariner (Part), S. T. COLERIDGE
      Beyond the shadow of the ship . . .
            . . . flash of golden fire
            P.F.P II 172   P.LIFE IV 56
Animals' Houses, JAMES REEVES
      Of animals' houses
            PUF.Q 75   REE.W.M 25
The Dismantled Ship, WALT WHITMAN
      In some unused lagoon, some nameless bay
            M.R.CHA 64

The Fly, WALTER DE LA MARE
 How large unto the tiny fly

Good Taste, CHRISTOPHER LOGUE
 Travelling, a man met a tiger, so . . .

The Little Creature, WALTER DE LA MARE
 Twinkum, twankum, twirlum, twitch—

An Old Woman of the Roads, PADRAIC COLUM
 O, to have a little house!

Spring goeth all in white, ROBERT BRIDGES
 Spring goeth all in white

Stopping by Woods on a Snowy Evening, ROBERT FROST
 Whose woods these are I think I know

PAN

A Musical Instrument, ELIZABETH BARRETT BROWNING
 What was he doing, the great god Pan

PARADISE
See **Eden: Heaven**

PARODY

The Everlasting Percy, or Mr. Masefield on the Railway Centenary,
E. V. KNOX
I used to be a fearful lad
    KEY III 82   PENG.M.C 244   WHEEL I 144

Lessons on Maths, A SCHOOLCHILD
    Today we have square roots and yesterday
    (original, see **Wars: Training** Naming of parts)
        WHEEL IV 204

The Lincolnshire Poacher, EDWARD THOMAS
    I was not apprenticed nor ever dwelt in famous Lincolnshire
    (original, see **Poachers**)
        THO.GR 63

The Muse among the Motors, RUDYARD KIPLING
    See throughout
        KIP.INC 655–85

Sea Fever, E. V. MILNER
    Must I go down to the Sea again?
    (original, see PEG III 28)
        PEG III 29

The Streets of Laredo, LOUIS MACNEICE
    O early one morning I walked out like Agag
    (original, see **Cowboys**)
        CHER 309   FLA 111   RIS 112

The Voice of the Lobster, LEWIS CARROLL
    'Tis the voice of the Lobster, I heard him declare
    (original, see **Laziness,** The Sluggard)
        KEY II 44

PARROTS

The Parrot: A True Story, THOMAS CAMPBELL
    A parrot, from the Spanish Main
        KEY I 107

PARSNIPS

The Parsnip, OGDEN NASH
   The parsnip, children, I repeat
   NA.P.B 159   WEALTH 25

PEACE

Down by the Riverside, ANON
   I'm going to lay down my heavy load
   A.F.B 50 (G)   PENG.A.F.S 144 (G,P)

Peace, HENRY VAUGHAN
   My soul, there is a country
      CHER 347   D.P.F.F 181   ECHO III 94
      EX.T.CH 185   FAB.C.V 368   OX.V.J III 85
      WEALTH 288

Peace Time, RALPH KNEVET
   The helmet now an hive for bees becomes
      OX.V.J IV 21

PEDLARS

Fine knacks for ladies, JOHN DOWLAND
   Fine knacks for ladies
      S.T.S II 76 (G,P)

The Pedlar leaves the Bar Parlour at Dymchurch, F. M. FORD
   Good-night, we'd best be jogging on
      OX.V.J III 51

The Pedlar's Caravan, W. B. RANDS
   I wished I lived in a caravan
      TREE I 69

There was a little woman, ANON
   There was a little woman
      FAB.N.V I 50   F.Y.D 91   G.TR.P 103
      M.R.FEEL 73   MY 78   P.LIFE III 53
      PUF.N.R 142   TOM.T.G 69   TREE II 54

PEGASUS

Pegasus, ELEANOR FARJEON
From the blood of Medusa
MY 39

PELICANS

The Pelican Chorus, EDWARD LEAR
King and Queen of the Pelicans we
PENG.AN 240   PENG.M.C 154

PENGUINS

Peter and Percival, E. V. RIEU
Peter and Percival lived in a place
PUF.Q 125

PESSIMISTS

The Pessimist, BEN KING
Nothing to do but work

BL.J IV 41	MY 92	OX.P.C 14
PENG.COM 177	R.R 132	V.F 89
WEALTH 22		

PETS
See also **Animals: Birds: Fishes & Sea Creatures**

My brother Bert, TED HUGHES
Pets are the hobby of my brother Bert
HU.MEET 25   WHEEL I 165

PEWITS

Two Pewits, EDWARD THOMAS
Under the after-sunset sky
COME 113   THO.GR 38

PHOTOGRAPHS
Waiting for the Birdie, OGDEN NASH
    Some hate broccoli, some hate bacon
        KEY I 102

PHYSICAL ACTIVITY
See also **Games: Sport**
See also **Bathing: Bicyling: Dancing: Digging: Fighting:
    Laughing: Marching: Mountaineering: Riding: Row-
    ing: Skating: Skipping: Walking**

Things, WILLIAM JAY SMITH
    Trains are foɪ going
        V.F 155

PIGEONS
Mrs. Peck-Pigeon, ELEANOR FARJEON
    Mrs. Peck-Pigeon
        F.FEET 72   P.LIFE I 47

Pigeons, RICHARD KELL
    They paddle with staccato feet
        HERE 53

PIGS
P was a pig, EDWARD LEAR
    P was a pig
        P.LIFE I 53

The Pigs and the Charcoal Burner, WALTER DE LA MARE
    The old pig said to the little pigs
        DE LA M.P II 205   F.FEET 86   IRON I 106
        OX.V.J II 37

The site: choose a dry site, R. DUNCAN
    The site: choose a dry site
        ALB I 61   M.CENT 37

The Temptation of St. Anthony, FRENCH TRANS GALES
    Goblins came, on mischief bent
        PENG.AN 247
Tom he was a Piper's Son, ANON
    Tom, he was a piper's son
        BL.J II 33   OX.N.R 164   PUF.N.R 168
Tom, Tom, the Piper's Son, ANON
    Tom, Tom the piper's son
        OX.N.R 46   PUF.N.R 17   TREE II 14
View of a Pig, TED HUGHES
    The pig lay on a barrow dead
        FLA 194   HERE 54   PENG.AN 248

PIKE

The Pike, EDMUND BLUNDEN
    From shadows of rich oaks outpeer
        ALB II 21   DAY 69   MOD 168
        PENG.AN 253   PENG.C.V 136   PENG.NEW 168
        P.F.P I 130   WHEEL III 168
Pike, TED HUGHES
    Pike in all part, green tigering the gold
        PENG.AN 254

PILGRIMS

To be a Pilgrim, JOHN BUNYAN
    Who would true valour see
        AN.SPO I 100   C.MUSE 293   P.SING 162
        R.R 160

PINES

The Pines, ANDREW YOUNG
    The eye might fancy that those pines
        YOU.P 43

PIPERS

The Pied Piper of Hamelin, ROBERT BROWNING
Hamelin Town's in Brunswick

B.P III 18	DRUM 17	ECHO I 25
EX.T.CH 127	FAB.C.V 160	G.TR.P 153
P.F.P I 70	P.SING 91	SPIR I 11

A Piper, S. O'SULLIVAN
A piper in the streets today

AN.SPO I 140	BL.J III 51	B.P II 43
COME 197	M.R.FEEL 26	

The Piper o' Dundee, ANON
The Piper came to our town

OX.V.J II 82	PEG II 59	P.P.TALK 33

Tom, he was a Piper's son, ANON
Tom, he was a piper's son

BL.J II 33	OX.N.R 164	PUF.N.R 168

Tom, the Piper's son, ANON
Tom, Tom, the piper's son

OX.N.R 46	PUF.N.R 17	TREE II 14

PIRATES

Captain Kidd, R. AND S. VINCENT BENÉT
This person in the gaudy clothes

P.LIFE III 11

Captain Kidd, ANON
My name was Robert Kidd

F.S.N.A 15 (G)

The Coasts of High Barbary, ANON
Look ahead, look astern, look the weather and the lee

FIRE.F.S 166 (P)	KEY III 113	OX.P.C 50

A Dutch Picture, H. W. LONGFELLOW
Simon Danz has come home again

P.SING 104	SPIR 18

Henry Martin, ANON
>   In merry Scotland, in merry Scotland
>   BAL 615   MER 189
>   There were three brothers in merry Scotland
>   IVES 46 (G,P)

The Inchcape Rock, ROBERT SOUTHEY
>   No stir in the air, no stir in the sea
>   AN.SPO I 29   CHER 141   EX.T.CH 170
>   G.TR.P 160   M.R.HAND 77   PEG I 64
>   P.P.OVER 29

The Pirate Don Durk of Dowdee, M. MEIGS
>   Ho for the pirate, Don Durk of Dowdee!
>   P.LIFE III 13

Spanish Gold, NORMAN LINDSAY
>   When I was young I used to hold
>   KEY III 22

PLANE-TREES

A London Plane-Tree, AMY LEVY
>   Green is the plane-tree in the square
>   WEALTH 260

PLANTS
See **Ferns: Flowers: Nettles: Vegetables**

PLOUGHING

Late Autumn, ANDREW YOUNG
>   The boy called to his team
>   KEY IV 38   YOU.P 32

The Painful Plough, ANON
>   O Adam was a ploughboy when ploughing first began
>   OX.S.M.P 24 (M)

POLITICS

See also **Freedom Songs: Human Rights: Protests (Political): Refugees**

Emperors of the Island, DANNIE ABSE
> There is the story of a deserted island
>> DAWN 87   DAY 99

The Gondoliers (Part), W. S. GILBERT
> There lived a king, as I've been told
>> P.P.FAL 96

PONDS

Our Pond, DANIEL PETTIWARD
> I am fond
>> WHEEL II 162

PONIES

See **Horses & Ponies**

POPLARS

The Poplar Field, WILLIAM COWPER
> The poplars are felled; farewell to the shade
>> COME 49

The Poplars, CLIVE SANSOM
> Where the moorland ends and the oakwood glooms
>> AN.SPO I 148

PORTRAITS

See also OX.N.R 81–102 (for the youngest): HU.MEET throughout
See also **Boys: Children: Egoists: Families: Famous People: Girls: Optimists: Pessimists: Teenagers: Trades & Professions**

John Gilpin, WILLIAM COWPER
> John Gilpin was a citizen
>> A.B.L.P 350   CH.GAR I 58   D.P.ROAD 119
>> P.P.FACT 55   V.F 39   WEALTH 101

Lazy Man's Song, CHINESE TRANS WALEY
    I could have a job, but am too lazy to choose it
        HAP 72   WAL.C.P 139

Love Poem, JOHN F. NIMS
    My clumsiest dear, whose hands shipwreck vases
        PEG V 47   PENG.M.A.V 278

Lucy Lake, OGDEN NASH
   Lawsamassy, for heaven's sake !
        NA.P.B 96

The Man in the Bowler Hat, A. S. TESSIMOND
    I am the unnoticed, the unnoticeable man
        THEME 143

Meg Merrilies, JOHN KEATS
    Old Meg she was a Gipsy

A.D.L 133	AN.SPO II 106	ECHO I 55
EX.T.CH I 52	MER 293	M.R.ON 42
MY 88	OX.V.J II 41	P.LIFE IV 24
P.P.TALK 15	P.SING 87	PUF.V 235
R.R 124	THIS.W.D 137	

The Miller from *Canterbury Tales*, GEOFFREY CHAUCER
    The Miller was a stout carl for the nones
        M.M.A 53
    The Miller was a chap of sixteen stone
        M.M.A 54   WEALTH 209

Miniver Cheevy, E. A. ROBINSON
    Miniver Cheevy, child of scorn
        CHER 467   FAB.C.V 120   R.R 39

Miss Thompson goes Shopping, MARTIN ARMSTRONG
    In her lone cottage on the downs
        P.SING 121

Mistress Fell, GEOFFREY JOHNSON
    To hear tall Mistress Fell again
        ALB I 88

Mistress Margaret Hussey, JOHN SKELTON
 Merry Margaret, as midsummer flower
  FAB.C.V 116   P.W 52

Mr. Flood's Party, E. A. ROBINSON
 Old Eben Flood, climbing alone one night
  EV.M 69   OX.V.J IV 78

An Old Woman of the Roads, PADRAIC COLUM
 Oh, to have a little house !
  EX.T.CH 148   SCH.M.V 31

Portrait of a Romantic, A. S. J. TESSIMOND
 He is in love with the land that is always over
  PEG V 92

Sir Smasham Uppe, E. V. RIEU
 Good afternoon, Sir Smasham Uppe
  D.P.ROAD 139 PEG I 20   P.LIFE IV 88
  PUF.Q 115   V.F 121

Skipper, C. FOX SMITH
 A rough old nut
  A.D.L 128

The Squire from *Canterbury Tales*, GEOFFREY CHAUCER
 With him ther was his sone, a yong Squyer
  P.W 45   R.R 119
 He had his son with him, a fine young Squire
  WEALTH 211

Thrushes, HUMBERT WOLFE
 The City Financier
  B.P II 49   OX.V.J III 29 P.LIFE III 72

To my mother, GEORGE BARKER
 Most near, most dear, most loved and most far
  FAB.M.V 332 M.P.W 4   PENG.C.V 263

PRAYERS

See also **Graces**

For Sleep or Death, RUTH PITTER
     Cure me with quietness

God be in my head, ANON
     God be in my head

A House Blessing, W. CARTRIGHT
     Saint Francis and Saint Benedight

Matthew, Mark, Luke and John, ANON
     Matthew, Mark, Luke and John

Prayer before Birth, LOUIS MACNEICE
     I am not yet born: oh hear me

The Robin's Song, ANON
     God bless the field and bless the furrows

Song of a Hebrew, DANNIE ABSE
     Working is another way of praying

When wilt Thou save the People? E. ELLIOTT
     When wilt Thou save the people?

PRISON
See also **Hanging**

The Knight in Prison, WILLIAM MORRIS
    Wearily, drearily
       P.REM 96

PRISONERS

The Prisoner, CHINESE TRANS WALEY
    Tartars led in chains
       WAL.C.P 126

PROFESSIONS
See **Trades & Professions**

PROTESTS
See also **Curses: Freedom Songs**

PROTESTS (PERSONAL)

Lines to a Don, H. BELLOC
    Remote and ineffectual don
       BEL.S.V 91   PENG.COM 174

The Oxford Voice, D. H. LAWRENCE
    When you hear it languishing
       LAW.PENG 138   PENG.COM 179

PROTESTS (POLITICAL)

The Durham Lock-Out (1892), ANON
    In our Durham County I am sorry for to say
       C.MUSE 189

The Fine Old English Gentleman (1841), CHARLES DICKENS
    I'll sing you a new ballad and I'll warrant it first-rate
       C.MUSE 181   FAB.BAL 185

PUBLIC LIBRARY

PUCK
See **Robin Goodfellow**

PUNCH & JUDY

PUNISHMENT
See **Hanging: Transportation**

PUPPIES

Stormy, W. CARLOS WILLIAMS
> What name could
>> PENG.AN 273

QUAILS
Quail's Nest, JOHN CLARE
> I wandered out one rainy day
>> BL.J III 36   EX.T.CH 16

QUARRELS
Discord in Childhood, D. H. LAWRENCE
> Outside the house an ashtree hung its terrible whips
>> THEME 73

QUEENS
See **Kings & Queens: England (History)**

QUESTION & ANSWER
All's Well, ANON
> A friend of mine was married to a scold
>> KEY IV 138

Betty and her Ducks, ANON
> Oh! Betty, Betty, have you seen my ducks today?
>> KEY II 82

Edward, Edward, ANON
> Why does your brand sae drop wi' blude?

AN.SPO II 9	BAL 86	BUN 39
COM 108	COME 430	FAB.BAL 119
IRON I 72	KEY I 19	PEG III 89
P.F.P I 149	P.P.TALK 72	P.W 4
WHEEL III 25		

> What makes that blood on the point of your knife?
>> ECHO II 49   IVES 48 (G,P)
> What bluid's that on thy coat lap?
>> BAL 85

The Fause Knight upon the Road, ANON
Meet on the Road
> O where are ye gaun?

BUN 84	COME 334	EX.T.H 29
FAB.C.V 105	KEY IV 92	MER 122
M.M.A 30	OX.L.V 98	OX.P.C 84
OX.V.J II 33	P.F.P I 56	P.TONG 99
PUF.V 205	TREE IV 116	

The Ferryman, CHRISTINA ROSSETTI
> Ferry me across the water

M.R.FEEL 24	TREE II 52

The Keys of Canterbury, ANON
> O Madam I will give to you the keys of Canterbury

KEY III 104

Lord Randal, ANON
> O where hae ye been, Lord Randal my son?

BAL 81	FAB.BAL 34	IVES 58 (G,P)
M.R.HAND 72	OX.V.J IV 22	P.F.P I 147
P.P.TALK 74	P.TONG 101	P.W. 16
R.R 26		

My Man John, ANON
> My man John, what can the matter be?

KEY III 101

Overheard on a Saltmarsh, HAROLD MUNRO
> Nymph, nymph, what are your beads?

COME 124	PEG I 94	P.F.P I 110
THIS.W.D 33		

The Quarry, W. H. AUDEN
> O what is that sound which so thrills the ear?

AUD.PENG 27	DAWN 42	M.R.CHA 54
P.F.P I 170	WHEEL III 180	

Quite a History, ARLO BATES
    Where have you been, Lysander Pratt?
        KEY IV 140

The Saucy Sailor, ANON
    Come my own one, come my fond one
        KEY III 24

Soldier, Soldier, RUDYARD KIPLING
    Soldier, soldier, come from the wars
        KIP.INC 394

Soldier, Soldier, ANON
    Soldier, soldier, won't you marry me?
        D.P.JOU 98   EX.T.TRO 74   MER 142
        OX.L.V 363   OX.P.C 35   OX.S.M.J II 10 (M)
        PUF.N.R 176   S.N.W 38 (G,P)

What's in there? ANON
    What's in there?
        TREE II 77

What's your name? ANON
    What's your name?
        TREE I 37

Which? WALTER DE LA MARE
    What did you say?
        DE LA M.CH 100

Why so pale and wan? SIR JOHN SUCKLING
    Why so pale and wan, fond lover?
        R.R 142

RABBITS

Done For, WALTER DE LA MARE
    Old Ben Bailey
        TREE I 24

H

The Snare, JAMES STEPHENS
> I hear a sudden cry of pain

AN.METH 201	COME 96	D.P.JOU 20
EX.T.CH 20	F.FEET 129	MOD 104
MY 129	OX.P.C 130	P.F.P I 95
P.LIFE II 25	SCH.M.V 161	SPIR 45
TREE IV 71		

To see the Rabbit, ALAN BROWNJOHN
> We are going to see the rabbit

HAP 36	JA.PO 15	PENG.AN 261

The White Rabbit, E. V. RIEU
> He is white as Helvellyn when winter is well in

> MY 164

RACE
See also **Eskimos: Foreigners: Freedom Songs**

Black Boy in a New World, A SCHOOLCHILD
> Here am I a lonely boy

> WHEEL II 182

The Little Black Boy, WILLIAM BLAKE
> My mother bore me in the southern wild

BLA.P 67	BLA.PENG 28	CH.GAR 172
COM 40	COME 22	MER 291
P.REM 34	P.W 139	WHEEL II 71

A Strange Meeting, W. H. DAVIES
> The moon is full and so am I

M.R.CHA 31	OX.P.C 148	P.REM 114

RACING (HORSES)

At the Races: the Starter, ALAN ROSS
> They're off!

> KEY IV 84

RAMS
See **Sheep**

RAT-RACE

RATS

The Rat, ANDREW YOUNG
>   Strange that you let me come so near
>> WEALTH 70   YOU.P 69

Rats, FRANK EYRE
>   When dusk is falling
>> KEY I 42

Song of the Brown Sea Rat, HAMISH MACLAREN
>   Now we are the rodent mariners
>> AN.SPO I 128

RAVENS

The Corbie and the Crow, ANON
>   The Corbie with his roupie throat
>> P.P.TALK 61

The Raven, EDGAR ALLAN POE
>   Once upon a midnight dreary,
>>   while I pondered weak and weary
>> COME 320

The Three Ravens, ANON
>   There were three ravens sat on a tree
>> BAL I I I   C.S.B 88 (P)   FAB.BAL 37
>> FIRE.F.S 94 (P)

The Twa Corbies / Ravens, ANON
>   As I was walking all alane
>> BAL I 12   BUN I 32   COME I09
>> FAB.BAL 38   MER 24I   PEG II 64
>> P.F.P I 147   PUF.V 98   P.W 6
>> R.R I70

READING

Readers and Riders, EMILY DICKINSON
>   There is no frigate like a book
>> OX.V.J III 9

REAPING
See **Harvest**

RED INDIANS
See **Indians, Red**

REFLECTION

A Thought, W. H. DAVIES
> When I look into a glass
>> P.TIME 119

REFUGEES

The Little Cart, CH'ÊN TZU-LUNG TRANS WALEY
> The little cart jolting and banging
>> through the yellow haze of dusk
>> WAL.C.P 199

The Quarry, W. H. AUDEN
> Oh what is that sound which so thrills the ear?

AUD.PENG 27	DAWN 42	M.R.CHA 54
P.F.P I 170	WHEEL III 180	

Refugee Blues, W. H. AUDEN
> Say this city has ten million souls

ALB II 5	EV.M 58	FLA 106
THEME 86	UNDER 46	WEALTH 250

Refugees, A SCHOOLCHILD
> Of course I'll do what I can, but—
>> WHEEL IV 211

RELIGIOUS THEMES
See also **Blessings: Church-Going: Heaven: Pilgrims: Praise: Prayers: Saints: Spirituals**

RELIGIOUS THEMES (NEW TESTAMENT)
See **Christ: Christmas (Religious): Crucifixion: Dives & Lazarus: Easter: Epiphany: Herod: Martha: Saints**

RELIGIOUS THEMES (OLD TESTAMENT)
See **Creation: Daniel: David: Eden: Eve: Jacob: Jonah: Joseph: Joshua: Moses: Naaman: Noah: Samson**

RELIGIOUS THEMES

All but Blind, WALTER DE LA MARE
All but blind

      DE LA M.CH 144   R.R 168

Design, ROBERT FROST
I found a dimpled spider, fat and white

      FRO.P 396   FRO.PENG 194   THEME 3

Eddi's Service (A.D. 687); RUDYARD KIPLING
Eddi, priest of St. Wilfrid

      KEY III 148   KIP.INC 503   M.R.HAND 100
      P.P.TALK 55

Love, GEORGE HERBERT
Love bade me welcome, yet my soul drew back

      CHER 433   COME 483   PENG.E.V 113

REPTILES
See **Snakes: Tortoises: Turtles**

REVENGE

Heriot's Ford, RUDYARD KIPLING
What's that that hirples at my side?

      KIP.INC 643   P.F.P I 169

REVENGE, THE

The Revenge, LORD TENNYSON
At Flores in the Azores Sir Richard Grenville lay

      D.P.WAY 106   ECHO I 7   FAB.C.V 247
      PEG II 36   P.F.P II 57   P.P.OVER 56
      P.REM 70   PUF.V 87

RHYMES
See **Alphabet Rhymes: Counting Rhymes: Counting-Out Rhymes: Ruthless Rhymes**

RIDDLES
See also **Ballads, Riddling**

See B.B.F 192	CHER 3, 10, 11, 12, 36, 97, 235, 389, 395, 402
FAB.N.V 48–54	MER 135–7, 164, 235, 254, 296, 329
MY 25	OX.N.R 147–55, 197
P.P.SAL 12, 13, 18	PUF.N.R 72–5
TOM.T.G 31–2	TREE I 54–5, 68

A E I O U, JONATHAN SWIFT
We are very little creatures

MER 252	P.REM 38	TOM.T.G 28
TREE IV 81	WHEEL I 54	

The Devil's Nine Questions, ANON
O you must answer my questions nine

F.S.N.A 180 (G,B)   IVES 38 (G,P)

An Egg, ANON
In marble halls as white as milk
P.P.BELL 24

The Exeter Book (Part), ANON TRANS K. C. HOLLAND
The deep sea suckled me, the waves sounded over me
PENG.AN 229

A Head but no Hair, CHRISTINA ROSSETTI
A pin has a head but has no hair
KEY II 51

A Long-Eared Beast, JONATHAN SWIFT
A long-eared beast and a field-house for cattle
KEY II 91

Pery Mery Winkle Domine, ANON
I had four sisters sailed across the sea
KEY I 89

Riddle on the Moon and Sun, ANGLO–SAXON TRANS BONE
    I saw a creature sally with beauty
        P.W 31

The Riddle Song, ANON
    I gave my love a cherry without a stone
        A.F.B 72 (G)   FIRE.F.S 25 (P)   IVES 36 (G,P)
        S.N.W 48 (G,P)
    I'll give my love an apple without e'er a core
        F.S.N.A 27 (G,B)   KEY I 88   M.R.HAND 5
    My love sent me a chicken with ne'er a bone
        OX.N.R 197

Spells, JAMES REEVES
    I dance and dance without any feet
        KEY I 90

RIDING
See also **Horses: Racing (Horses)**

A Farmer went Trotting, ANON
    A farmer went trotting upon his grey mare
        BL.J I 30   P.LIFE I 12

How they brought the Good News from Ghent to Aix,
ROBERT BROWNING
    I sprang to the stirrup, and Joris and he;
        G.TR.P 149   M.R.ON 14   PEG II 53
        P.REM 89   SPIR 29   WEALTH 146

The Pursuit, G. W. THORNBURY
    Trample! Trample! went the roan
        M.R.ON 26

RISING EARLY

An Early Levée, CHINESE TRANS WALEY
    At Chang-an—a full foot of snow
        WAL.C.P 134

RIVERS
See also **Thames**

Clear and Cool, CHARLES KINGSLEY
 Clear and cool, clear and cool
  KEY III 77

The River's Tale, RUDYARD KIPLING
 Twenty bridges from Tower to Kew
  KEY III 78   KIP.INC 689

Sabrina Fair, JOHN MILTON
 Sabrina Fair
  CH.GAR 32   COME I 30   ECHO II 106
  FAB.C.V 217

The Two Rivers, ANON
 Says Tweed to Till
  BUN 83   CHER 165   COME 425
  FAB.C.V 268   P.P.OVER 24 TREE IV 32

ROBIN GOODFELLOW

Robin Goodfellow, BEN JONSON
 From Oberon in Fairyland
  MER 313

ROBINS

The Death and Burial of Cock Robin, ANON
 Who killed Cock Robin?
  F.S.N.A 181 (G,B) G.TR.P 62   MER 9
  OX.L.V 284   OX.N.R 166   P.P.SAL 41
  PUF.N.R 76   PUF.V 38   TOM.T.G 41
  TREE I 40

The Red Robin, JOHN CLARE
 Cock Robin, he got a new tippet in spring
  MER 221

A Roundabout by the Sea, JOHN H. WALSH
  The crimson-spotted horses
    EX.T.TRO 30

ROWING

Michael, row the boat ashore, ANON
  Michael, row the boat ashore
    A.F.B 75 (G)

RUNNYMEDE

The Reeds of Runnymede, RUDYARD KIPLING
  At Runnymede, at Runnymede
    KIP.INC 695

RUTHLESS RHYMES

Aunt Eliza, HARRY GRAHAM
  In the drinking well
    CHER 470

Opportunity, HARRY GRAHAM
  When Mrs. Gorm (Aunt Eloise)
    P.P.WIDE 109

The Stern Parent, HARRY GRAHAM
  Father heard his children scream
    CHER 470

Uncle, HARRY GRAHAM
  Uncle, whose inventive brain
    V.F 68

SAILORS
See also **Pirates: Smugglers**
See also **Benbow: Columbus: Drake: Grenville: Kidd: Nelson**

The Ancient Mariner, S. T. COLERIDGE
  It is an ancient mariner
    A.B.L.P 425   WEALTH 113

The Goole Captain, LEONARD CLARK
> One day as I walked by Crocodile Mansions
>> DAWN 34

Johnny Todd, ANON
> Johnny Todd he took a notion
>> S.T.S II 14 (G,P)

The Last Chantey (1892), RUDYARD KIPLING
> Thus saith the Lord in the vault above the Cherubim
>> FAB.C.V 323   KIP.INC 160

Luck, WILFRID GIBSON
> What bring you, sailor, home from the sea?
>> OX.V.J II 21

The Old Sailor, A. A. MILNE
> There was once an old sailor my grandfather knew
>> B.P II 51   FAB.N.V 36   MIL.N.S 37
>> SCH.M.V II4

Psalm 107, THE BIBLE
> They that go down to the sea in ships
>> P.SING I

Seumas Beg, JAMES STEPHENS
> A man was sitting underneath a tree
>> OX.V.J III 10

Skipper, C. FOX SMITH
> A rough old nut
>> A.D.L 128

Skipper Ireson's Ride, J. G. WHITTIER
> Of all the rides since the birth of time
>> SPIR 72

A Truthful Song II, RUDYARD KIPLING
> I tell this tale which is strictly true
>> KIP.INC 635

SAILORS' SONGS
See also **Sea Shanties**

Heart of Oak, DAVID GARRICK
    Come cheer up, my lads, 'tis to glory we steer
        OX.S.M.J III 17

Lord Arnaldos, J. F. FLECKER
    The strangest of adventures
        OX.V.J IV 9

Roll down to Rio, RUDYARD KIPLING
    I've never sailed the Amazon
        KIP.INC 588   M.R.FEEL 44   PEG I 57

Song of the Galley Slaves, RUDYARD KIPLING
    We pulled for you when the wind was against us
      and the sails were low
        CHER 223

SAINTS: ST. JEROME

St. Jerome and the Lion, RUMER GODDEN
    To Bethlehem, with its white stone and towers
        GOD.JER I

SAINTS: ST. MARTIN

St. Martin and the Beggar, THOM GUNN
    Martin sat young upon his bed
        AN.WAI 122

SAINTS: ST. PAUL

At his execution, RUDYARD KIPLING
    I am made all things to all men
        KIP.INC 761

In the British Museum, THOMAS HARDY
  What do you see in that time-touched stone?
    HAR.PENG 118   HAR.SEL 63

SAINTS: ST. STEPHEN

Saint Stephen was a Clerk, ANON
  Saint Stephen was a clerk in King Herod's hall
    BAL 107   COME 240   P.P.OVER 63
    PUF.V 258   WHEEL I 19

SAMSON

How Samson bore away the gates of Gaza, VACHEL LINDSAY
  Once in a night as black as ink
    LIN.P 175

SCARECROWS

The Lonely Scarecrow, JAMES KIRKUP
  My poor old bones—I've only two
    DAWN 19   HAP 38   OX.P.C 139

The Scarecrow, WALTER DE LA MARE
  All winter through I bow my head
    DE LA M.CH 67   DE LA M.P. I 123   EX.T.CH 40
    OX.P.C 139   P.F.P II 27   P.SING 25
    TODAY 82

Scarecrow, ELEANOR FARJEON
  Hi, Mister Scarecrow!
    TREE III 11

SCHOLARS

The Learn'd Astronomer, WALT WHITMAN
  When I heard the learn'd astronomer
    R.R 72

The Scholars, W. B. YEATS
> Bald heads forgetful of their sins
>> PEG V 77   YEA.P 158

SCHOOL

Ask Daddy he won't know, OGDEN NASH
> Now that they've abolished chrome work
>> ALB I 119

Exercise Book, PRÉVERT TRANS DEHU
> Two and two four
>> EV.M 11   WEALTH 14

Last Lesson of the Afternoon, D. H. LAWRENCE
> When will the bell ring and end this weariness?
>> ALB I 94   UNDER 99

Lessons on Maths, A SCHOOLCHILD
> Today we have square roots and yesterday
> (original: see **Wars: 1939–45 (Training)**)
>> WHEEL IV 204

School's Out, HAL SUMMERS
> Four o'clock strikes
>> DAWN 28   HAP 70

School's Out, W. H. DAVIES
> Girls scream
>> BL.J I 1   MOD 65   P.TIME 68
>> TREE II 61

SCHOOLMASTERS

Pedagogue Arraigned, JOHN WAIN
> You lay across my childhood like a stone
>> PEG V 82

The Village Schoolmaster, OLIVER GOLDSMITH
> Beyond yon straggling fence that skirts the way
>> AN.SPO I 117

SCIENCE & SCIENTISTS
See also **Space Travel**

James Honeyman, W. H. AUDEN
> James Honeyman was a silent child
> > ALB I 6 MY 94 RIS 100

The Physicist, R. P. LISTER
> Where in the world I stand and gaze
> > PEG V I

SCORPIONS

The Scorpion, H. BELLOC
> The Scorpion is as black as soot
> > FAB.N.V 75

SCOTLAND

Charlie he's my darling, ANON
> An' Charlie he's my darling
> > P.P.OVER 12

The Flowers of the Forest, JANE ELLIOT
> I've heard them lilting at our ewe-milking
> > OX.S.M.P 23 (M) P.P.FAL 25 WEALTH 33

Johnnie Cope, ANON
> Cope sent a letter frae Dunbar
> > OX.S.M.J III 38 (M)

Over the Sea to Skye, R. L. STEVENSON
> Sing me a song of a lad that is gone
> > D.P.ROAD 84

Scots wha hae, ROBERT BURNS
> Scots, wha hae wi' Wallace bled
> > PEG II 58 WHEEL I 66

Skye Boat Song, HAROLD BOULTON
> Speed bonnie boat like a bird on the wing
> > FIRE.F.S 18 (P)

Wae's me for Prince Charlie, WILLIAM GLEN
    A wee bird cam' tae oor ha' door
        OX.S.M.S III 12 (M)

Will ye no come back again? LADY NAIRNE
    Bonny Charlie's noo awa'
        OX.S.M.J III 31 (M)

SEA
See also **Boats: Coral: Desert Islands: Fog: Mermaids &
Mermen: Pirates: Sailors: Shells: Ships: Shipwrecks:
Tides:Vikings: Waves**

SEA (LYRIC & DESCRIPTIVE)

All day hear the noise of waters, JAMES JOYCE
    All day hear the noise of waters
        FAB.C.V 330

A Conversation, from *Under Milk Wood* DYLAN THOMAS
    What seas did you see
        OX.V.J IV 14

Follow the Sea, C. FOX SMITH
    What is it makes a man follow the sea?
        JOY 116

Horses, CHRISTINA ROSSETTI
    The horses of the sea
        BL.J I 55   OX.V.J II 79   TREE II 27

The Main-deep, JAMES STEPHENS
    The long-rolling
        PEG V 23

The Sea, JAMES REEVES
    The sea is a hungry dog
        PUF.Q 82   REE.W.M 73

A Sea Dirge, LEWIS CARROLL
There are certain things—a spider, a ghost
KEY III 97

The Sound of the Wind, CHRISTINA ROSSETTI
The wind has such a rainy sound

M.R.FEEL 56	OX.P.C 58	OX.V.J II 79
P.LIFE I 71	P.REM 26	TREE I 29

A Wet Sheet and a Flowing Sea, ALLAN CUNNINGHAM
A wet sheet and a flowing sea
PEG IV 102

SEA (NARRATIVE)

The Coasts of High Barbary, ANON
Look ahead, look astern, look the weather and the lee
FIRE F.S. 166 (P)   KEY III 113   OX.P.C 50

Flannan Isle, W. W. GIBSON
Though three men dwell on Flannan Isle

AN.METH 84	COME 415	M.M.A 11
M.R.ON 89	OX.P.C 78	P.F.P II 219
R.R 29	TW.N 116	WEALTH 162

The Forsaken Merman, MATTHEW ARNOLD
Come, dear children, let us away

AN.E.P 146	AN.SPO I 32	CH.GAR 34
DRUM 41	EX.T.CH 174	FAB.C.V 325
MY 68	OX.P.C 59	OX.V.J III 57
P.F.P II 214	P.P.BRA 51	P.W 210
SPIR 121		

The Golden Vanity, ANON
A ship have I got in the North Country
OX.P.C 57

Last Chantey, RUDYARD KIPLING
Thus said the Lord in the vault above the Cherubim
FAB.C.V 323   KIP.INC 160

The Mermaid, ANON
    On Friday morn when we set sail
        B.P. III 72   COME 421   EX.T.CH 26
        P.F.P. I 57   TOM.T.G 130
    As we lay musing in our beds
        BAL 673

Sir Patrick Spens, ANON
    The king sits in Dunfermline town
        A.B.L.P 133   BAL 179   BUN I
        COME 425   D.P.ROAD 29   FAB.BAL 121
        FAB.C.V 296   OX.P.C 47   OX.V.J IV 16
        PEG II 32   P.F.P I 142   P.LIFE IV 61
        P.P.OVER 69   P.REM 100   PUF.V 99
        P.W 7   SPIR 134   WHEEL II 43

SEA BATTLES
See also **Armada: Benbow, Admiral: Grenville, Sir Richard: Lepanto: Revenge, The: Trafalgar**

Captain Death, ANON
    The muse with the hero's brave deeds being fired
        C.MUSE 232

The Famous Fight at Malago (1656), ANON
    Come all you brave sailors that sails on the main
        C.MUSE 80

The Shannon and the Chesapeake, ANON
    Now the Chesapeake so bold
        OX.S.M.P 26 (M)

SEA BIRDS

The Storm, WALTER DE LA MARE
    First there were two of us, then there were three of us
        AN.SPO I 130   DE LA M.CH 40

SEA MONSTERS
See also **Kraken: Leviathan**

Beowulf's Fight with the Sea Monster, TRANS SERRAILLIER
    The King saddled his war-steed, proud champion
        OX.V.J IV 10

Grim and Gloomy, JAMES REEVES
    Oh grim and gloomy
        PUF.Q 88   REE.W.M 17

Sea Serpent, ALBERTA VICKRIDGE
    Ten degrees south, a hundred east, at sea
        AN.SPO I 160

The Sea Serpent Chantey, VACHEL LINDSAY
    There's a snake on the western wave
        LIN.P 149

SEA SHANTIES
See also **Sailors' Songs**

As I walked down on Broadway, ANON
Can't you dance the Polka
    As I walked down on Broadway
        PENG.A.F.S 41 (G,P)
    As I came down the Bowery
        FIRE.F.S 160 (P)

Billy Boy, ANON
    Where have ye been all the day?
        KEY I 21   OX.N.R 189   OX.S.M.J I 43

Blow the Man Down, ANON
    Oh blow the man down, bullies, blow the man down
        A.F.B 39 (G)   FIRE.F.S 152(P)   IVES 130 (G,P)
        OX.S.M.J III 50

Blow ye winds in the morning, ANON
  As I walked out one morning to view the meadows round
    OX.S.M.P 25 (M,R)

Bound for the Rio Grande, ANON
  I'll sing you a song of the fish of the sea
    OX.S.M.S I 51

The Bullgine Run, ANON
  O the smartest skipper you can find
    F.S.N.A 56 (G,B,P)

The Drunken Sailor, ANON
  What shall we do with the drunken sailor?
    FIRE.F.S. 176 (P)   IVES 136 (G,P)   OX.S.M.J III 15 (M)

Leave her, Johnny, ANON
  I thought I heard the captain say
    D.P.WAY 118   KEY III 74
  O times are hard and wages are low
    S.T.S I 50 (G)

The Rio Grande, ANON
  O say were you ever in Rio Grande?
    FIRE.F.S 140 (P)

Sally Brown, ANON
  Sally Brown she's a bright mulatter
    OX.S.M.J II 32 (M)

Shenandoah, ANON
  O Shenandoah, I long to hear you
    A.F.B 17 (G)   B.L.A.F.S 138 (G,P)   FIRE.F.S 136 (P)
    F.S.N.A 53 (G,B)   IVES 134 (G,P)   PENG.A.F.S 40 (G,P)

Spanish Ladies, ANON
  Farewell and adieu to you fair Spanish Ladies
    P.P.WIDE 21

A Yankee Ship, ANON
    A Yankee ship came down the river
        KEY III 76   MER 362

SEALS

Lukannon, RUDYARD KIPLING
    I met my mates in the morning (and oh but I am old)
        KIP.INC 571

SEASIDE
See also **Bathing**

At the Seaside, R. L. STEVENSON
    When I was down beside the sea
        DRUM 39   M.R.FEEL 66

The Beach, ROBERT GRAVES
    Louder than gulls the little children scream
        GRA.PENG 148   M.CENT 30

maggie and milly and molly and may, E. E. CUMMINGS
    maggie and milly and molly and may
        CUM.PENG 81   HAP 18

The Pool in the Rock, WALTER DE LA MARE
    In this water, clear as air
        IRON I 80   KEY III 119   P.LIFE IV 9

The Rock Pool, EDWARD SHANKS
    This is the sea. In these uneven walls
        PEG IV 101

Seascape, FRANCES CORNFORD
    The liquid unhorizoned sea
        OX.V.J III 68

Shrimping, IAN SERRAILLIER
    I take my shrimping net, wade into the pool
        SER.HAP 23

SEASONS
See also **Autumn: Harvest: May Day: Months: Spring: Summer: Winter**

The Faerie Queene (Part), EDMUND SPENSER
>   So, forth issew'd the Seasons of the yeare
>   ECHO III 114

Round the Year, COVENTRY PATMORE
>   The crocus, while the days are dark
>   M.R.FEEL 47

Seasons, CHRISTINA ROSSETTI
>   O the cheerful budding time
>   TREE III 22

SEDGE-WARBLERS

Sedge-warblers, EDWARD THOMAS
>   Sedge-warblers, clinging so light
>   THO.GR 13

Sedge-warblers, EDWARD THOMAS
>   This beauty made me dream there was a time
>   THO.SEL 30

SENSES
See also **Food: Music: Noise: Smells: Sounds**

The Great Lover, RUPERT BROOKE
>   These I have loved
>   PEG III 4   R.R 131   WEALTH 222

Two Deep Clear Eyes, WALTER DE LA MARE
>   Two deep clear eyes
>   DE LA M.CH 142

SHAG

At Porthcothan, CHRISTOPHER MIDDLETON
>   A spectre of dark, at low tide on the tide-line
>   PENG.AN 271

SHAKESPEARE

The Coiner (c.1611), RUDYARD KIPLING
Against the Bermudas we foundered, whereby
KIP.INC 758

SHARKS

The Flattered Flying Fish, E. V. RIEU
Said the shark to the flying fish over the phone
B.P III 31   PUF.Q 122

The Maldive Shark, H. MELVILLE
About the shark, phlegmatical one
B.B.F 186   IRON II 1   R.R.177

The Shark, LORD ALFRED DOUGLAS
A treacherous monster is the shark
KEY III 100

SHEEP
See also **Lambs**

A Child's Pet, W. H. DAVIES
When I sailed out of Baltimore
COME 95   KEY II 56   P.LIFE III 79

The Derbyshire Ram, ANON
As I went down to Derby, sir, all on a market day
B.B.F 195   BL.J IV 23   ECHO II 8
FAB.N.V 70   KEY III 126   MER 173
OX.N.R. 205   PEG I 46   PENG.A.F.S 32 (G,P)
S.T.S I 18 (G)

Sheep, W. H. DAVIES
When I was once in Baltimore
D.P.JOU 21   KEY II 39   MER 322
M.R.ON 47   PEG I 45   P.LIFE III 78
P.REM 121

SHELLS

SHIPS
See also **Submarines**

SHIPS (LYRIC & DESCRIPTIVE)

Roll Down to Rio, RUDYARD KIPLING
I've never sailed the Amazon
KIP.INC 588   M.R.FEEL 44   PEG I 57

Song of the Galley Slaves, RUDYARD KIPLING
We pulled for you when the wind was against us
and the sails were low
CHER 223

SHIPS (NARRATIVE)

The Golden Vanity, ANON
A ship have I got in the North Country
OX.P.C 57

Minesweepers (1914–8), RUDYARD KIPLING
Dawn off the Foreland—the young flood making
KIP.INC 612

The Revenge, LORD TENNYSON
At Flores in the Azores Sir Richard Grenville lay
D.P.WAY 106   ECHO I 7   FAB.C.V 247
PEG II 36   P.F.P II 57   P.P.OVER 56
P.REM 70   PUF.V 87

The Ship of Rio, WALTER DE LA MARE
There was a ship of Rio
DE LA M.P II 125   EX.T.CH 76   FAB.N.V 242
OX.V.J I 66   P.LIFE III 19   P.P.FACT 70

SHIPWRECKS (LYRIC & DESCRIPTIVE)

Clarence's Dream, WILLIAM SHAKESPEARE
Methought I saw a thousand fearful wrecks
RICHARD III I iv 24   CHER 229   PEG V 107
P.W 70

The French Wars, RUDYARD KIPLING
The boats of Newhaven and Folkstone and Dover
KIP.INC 707

Full Fathom Five, WILLIAM SHAKESPEARE
Full fathom five thy father lies

TEMPEST I ii 394	AN.E.P 32	B.P II 53
CHER 231	COM 187	D.P.WAY 119
DRUM 39	ECHO I 24	FAB.C.V 268
KEY III 118	MER 270	MY 29
OX.V.J IV 89	PENG.E.V 67	P.F.P I 111
P.P.BRA 47	P.REM 202	P.W 65
THIS.W.D 83		

Patroling Barnegat, WALT WHITMAN
Wild wild the storm and the sea high running
KEY IV 88

The Wreck, W. W. GIBSON
She broke amidships: as the hull
KEY IV 88

SHIPWRECKS (NARRATIVE)

The Alice Jean, ROBERT GRAVES
One moonlight night a ship drove in
GRA.FID 54

The Inchcape Rock, ROBERT SOUTHEY
No stir in the air, no stir in the sea

AN.SPO I 29	CHER 141	EX.T.CH 170
G.TR.P 160	M.R.HAND 77	PEG I 64
P.P.OVER 29		

Sir Patrick Spens, ANON
The king sits in Dunfermline town

A.B.L.P 133	BAL 179	BUN I
COME 425	D.P.ROAD 29	FAB.BAL 121
FAB.C.V 296	OX.P.C 47	OX.V.J IV. 16
PEG II 32	P.F.P I 142	P.LIFE IV 61
P.P.OVER 69	P.REM 100	PUF.V 99
P.W 7	SPIR 134	WHEEL II 43

SHIV

Shiv and the Grasshopper, RUDYARD KIPLING
Shiv who poured the harvest and made the winds to blow
KIP.INC 507

SHOEMAKERS

No Tick, ANON
Mr. H. Spooner lives here
KEY III 66

Snobs, RICHARD CHURCH
I like a snob; I mean a mender of shoes
M.R.CHA 27

SHOOTING

Done For, WALTER DE LA MARE
Old Ben Bailey
TREE I 24

Hi!, WALTER DE LA MARE
Hi! Handsome hunting man
DE LE M.CH 132

The Wicked Fowler, PATRICK DICKINSON
The wicked fowler took his gun
TW.N 106

SHRIMPING

Shrimping, IAN SERRAILLIER
I take my shrimping net, wade into the pool
SER.HAP 23

SINGING

See also **Freedom Songs: Sailors' Songs: Sea Shanties: Soldiers' Songs: Work Songs**

Everyone Sang, S. SASSOON
Everyone suddenly burst out singing

A.D.L 214	AN.SPO I 148	MOD 121
MY 173	OX.V.J IV 107	P.SING 139

The Keel Row, ANON
>   As I came through Sandgate
>>   P.P TALK 12

The Quartette, WALTER DE LA MARE
>   Tom sang for joy and Ned sang for joy
>>   COM 39   DE LA M.P II 140

SISTERS

Goblin Market (Part), CHRISTINA ROSSETTI
>   Morning and evening
>>   P.F.P II 198   P.P.OVER 82

My Sister Jane, TED HUGHES
>   And I say nothing—no, not a word
>>   HAP 16   HU.MEET 13

SKATING

The Midnight Skaters, EDMUND BLUNDEN
>   The hop-poles stand in cones
>>   D.P.F.F 173   ECHO II 51   PENG.C.V 137
>>   P.TONG 133   R.R 28   SCH.M.V 13
>>   WEALTH 249

The Prelude (Part), WILLIAM WORDSWORTH
>   And in the frosty season, when the sun
>>   ECHO III 9   FAB.C.V 57   G.TR.P 281
>>   PEG III 25   P.TIME 165   P.W 150
>>   R.R 93
>   So through the darkness and the cold we flew
>>   COME 234

SKIPPING

Skipping, THOMAS HOOD
>   Little children skip
>>   TREE I 58

Skipping Song, JOHN WALSH
    When bread-and-cheese
        OX.V.J II 24

SLAVE TRADE

The Slave Chase (c.1850), ANON
    Set every stitch of canvas to woo the fresh'ning wind
        C.MUSE 142   KEY II 15

SLAVERY
See **U.S.A.: Slavery**

SLEEP
See **Falling Asleep: Lullabies**

SLOTHS

The Sloth, THEODORE ROETHKE
    In moving slow he has no peer
        HAP 73   PENG.AN 279   V.F I 30

SMELLS

Buying Fuel, RICHARD CHURCH
    Now I come to the farmer about some logs
        ALB I 38

Digging, EDWARD THOMAS
    Today I think
        THO.GR 28

Smells, CHRISTOPHER MORLEY
    Why is it that the poets tell
        D.P.F.F 46   JOY 118   PEG I 50
        P.LIFE IV 53

SMUGGLERS

Poor Honest Men (A.D. 1800), RUDYARD KIPLING
    Your jar of Virginny
        KIP. INC 537

Rum Lane, JAMES REEVES
    Gusty and chill
        KEY II 96

The Smuggler, ANON
    O my true love's a smuggler and sails upon the sea
        M.R.CHA 70

A Smuggler's Song, RUDYARD KIPLING
    If you wake at midnight and hear a horse's feet

B.P IV 47	D.P.JOU 72	EX.T.CH 117
KEY II 94	KIP.INC 636	M.R.ON 18
OX.V.J II 10	OX.P.C 52	PEG I 62
P.LIFE III 92	P.P.TALK 20	P.SING 78
SPIR 22		

SNAILS

The Garden Snail, R. WALLACE
    This backyard / cousin / to the octopus
        HAP 77

The Housekeeper, CHARLES LAMB
    The frugal snail, with forecast of repose
        PEG I 42

The Snail, JAMES REEVES
    At sunset, when the night-dews fall

BL.J IV 33	KEY I 32	RFE.W.M 3

The Snail, E. L. M. KING
    The horned snail so hates the drought
        TREE II 21

I

The Yellow Adder, A SCHOOLBOY
   The sun flows warm into the heather coves
      KEY IV 136

You Spotted Snakes, WILLIAM SHAKESPEARE
   You spotted snakes with double tongues

MIDSUMMER NIGHT'S DREAM II ii 9		B.B.F 165
B.P. IV 94	CH.GAR 18	D.P.JOU 103
EX.T.CH 28	F.FEET 157	G.TR.P 297
MER 367	MY 27	OX.V.J II 75
P.LIFE II 78	P.REM 40	P.SING 50
THIS.W.D 37	TREE II 32	

SNOW
See also **Thaw: Frost & Ice: Snowflakes**

Birds at Winter Nightfall, THOMAS HARDY
   Around the house the flakes fly faster
      HAR.SEL 28

Dust of Snow, ROBERT FROST
   The way a crow

FRO.P 270	FRO.PENG 142	FRO.YOU 86
IRON I 119	WEALTH 6	

Frying Pan's Theology, A. B. PATERSON
   Scene: On Monaro
      FAB.N.V 35

London Snow, ROBERT BRIDGES
   When men were all asleep the snow came flying

A.D.L 63	CHER 308	COME 234
PEG III 54	P.F.P II 43	WEALTH 258

The Pines, ANDREW YOUNG
   The eye might fancy that those pines
      YOU.P 43

White Fields, JAMES STEPHENS
  In the winter-time we go
        EX.T.H 81   TREE III 30

Winter, WALTER DE LA MARE
  Green Mistletoe
        CHER 394   DE LA M.CH 51   DE LA M.P I 96

Winter Snowstorm, JOHN CLARE
  Winter is come in earnest, and the snow
        IRON I 130

SNOWFLAKES

The Snowflake, WALTER DE LA MARE
  Before I melt
        A.D.L 16   B.P IV 14   PEG I 111

To a Snowflake, FRANCIS THOMPSON
  What heart could have thought you
        PEG V 43

SNOWMEN

The Snowman, WALTER DE LA MARE
  What shape is this in cowl of snow?
        DE LA M.CH 69

SOLDIERS
See also **Napoleon: War**

Danny Deever, RUDYARD KIPLING
  'What are the bugles blowin' for?' said Files-on-Parade
        FAB.BAL 195   KIP.INC 390   MOD 42
        OX.L.V 491   PEG IV 92   P.P.WIDE 96
        TW.N 58

Jimmy's Enlisted, ANON
  Oh, what's the matter with you, my lass?
        C.MUSE 239

Johnny has gone for a soldier, ANON
> There I sit on Butternut Hill
>> B.L.A.F.S 117 (G,P)   FIRE.F.S 69 (P)   IVES 98 (G,P)
>> S.N.W 23 (G,P)
> O Johnny dear has gone away
>> F.S.N.A 47 (G,B,P)

An Old Soldier of the Queen's, ANON
> Of an old soldier of the Queen's
>> KEY IV 58   P.W 21

The Soldier's Death, ANNE FINCH
> Trail all your pikes, dispirit every drum
>> R.R 46

SOLDIERS' SONGS

The British Grenadiers, ANON
> Some talk of Alexander, and some of Hercules
>> FIRE.F.S 198 (P)

The Duke of Plaza-Toro's Song, W. S. GILBERT
> In enterprise of martial kind
>> KEY II 34

Rimini, RUDYARD KIPLING
> When I left Rome for Lalage's sake
>> KIP.INC 536

Roman Wall Blues, W. H. AUDEN
> Over the heather the wet wind blows
>> AUD.PENG 46   DAWN 43   MY 79
>> PEG V 95   PENG.COM 302   WEALTH 250

The Song of the Western Men, R. S. HAWKER
> A good sword and a trusty hand
>> MER 225   M.R.ON 11   OX.S.M.J III 8 (M)
>> P.P.FACT 39

A Song to Mithras, RUDYARD KIPLING
  Mithras, God of the morning, our trumpets waken the wall
    KIP.INC 511   P.P.OVER 92

We be the King's Men, THOMAS HARDY
  We be the King's Men, hale and hearty
    COME 175   DRUM 15   EX.T.CH 105
    MER 346   M.R.FEEL 27   TOM.T.G 137

SOUNDS
See also **Noise**

Pleasant Sounds, JOHN CLARE
  The rustling of leaves under the feet in woods
    and under hedges
    KEY I 104   P.W 185

Regent's Park Terrace, BERNARD SPENCER
  The noises round my house. On cobbles bounding
    R.R 71

SOUTH AFRICA
See P.SING 164–97 for poems about South Africa by South
  Africans

SOWING

Sowing, EDWARD THOMAS
  It was a perfect day
    A.D.L 264   OX.V.J IV 84   PEG IV 49
    SCH.M.V 168   THO.GR 29

SPACE TRAVEL

Space Travellers, JAMES NIMMO
  There was a witch, hump-backed and hooded
    OX.V.J III 79

Tea in a Space Ship, JAMES KIRKUP
   In this world a tablecloth need not be laid
      ALB I 91   PEG V 12   PENG.C.V 344

SPARROWS

Phylip Sparrow, JOHN SKELTON
   When I remember again
      B.B.F 135

SPELLS
See **Charms & Spells**

SPIDERS

Low Love Life, IVOR C. F. TREBY
   The female spider
      PENG.YET 83

The Spider, JOHN CLARE
   The mottled spider, at eve's leisure, weaves
      KEY I 92

The Spider, ANDREW YOUNG
   A single white dewdrop
      YOU.P 50

SPIRITUALS
See also **Freedom Songs**

Des Bones Gwine to Rise Again, ANON
   De Lord he thought he'd make a man
      KEY IV 26

Didn't my Lord deliver Daniel?, ANON
   Didn't my Lord deliver Daniel?
      OX.S.M.S III 16   PENG.A.F.S 136 (G,P)

Down by the Riverside, ANON
 I'm goin' to lay down my heavy load
   A.F.B 50 (G)   PENG.A.F.S 144 (G,P)

Go Down, Moses, ANON
 When Israel was in Egypt land
   B.L.A.F.S 372 (G,P) FIRE.F.S 316 (P) PENG.A.F.S 138
                         (G,P)

Great Day. ANON
 Great Day
   PENG.A.F.S 140 (G,P)

Joshua fit de battle ob Jericho, ANON
 Joshua fit de battle ob Jericho
   A.F.B 37 (G)   FIRE.F.S 304 (P)

Little David, ANON
 David was a shepherd boy
   OX.S.M.J III 43 (M) PENG.A.F.S 126 (G,P)

Michael, row the boat ashore, ANON
 Michael, row the boat ashore
   A.F.B 75 (G)

My Lord, what a morning, ANON
 My Lord, what a morning
   FIRE.F.S 314 (P)

Oh, Mary don't you weep, ANON
 If I could I surely would
   A.F.B 78 (G)

Set down, servant, ANON
 'Set down, servant.' 'I cain' set down'
   B.L.A.F.S 362 (G,P)

Sometimes I feel like a motherless child, ANON
 Sometimes I feel like a motherless child
   A.F.B 49 (G)   B.L.A.F.S 368 (G,P)

Steal Away, ANON
>   Steal away, steal away
>   FIRE.F.S 298 (P)

Swing low, sweet chariot, ANON
>   Swing low, sweet chariot
>   A.F.B 16 (G)   ECHO III 118   FIRE.F.S 310 (P)
>   OX.S.M.S III 17 (M)

SPORT
See **Boxing: Cricket: Fishing: Football: Golf: Hunting: Physical Activity: Racing: Shooting: Tennis**

SPRING
See also **Months: Weather**

Beggar's Song, RICHARD BROME
>   Come! Come away! the Spring
>   EX.T.CH 23

Chanson Innocente, E. E. CUMMINGS
>   In Just—/spring
>   CUM.PENG I   EV.M 93   FAB.N.V 25
>   G.TR.P 272   HAP 67   PENG.M.A.V 179
>   THIS.W.D 69

Cuckoos, ANDREW YOUNG
>   When coltsfoot withers and begins to wear
>   KEY III 112   M.P.W 102   M.R.ON 62
>   PENG.AN 81   YOU.P 169

Description of Spring, EARL OF SURREY
>   The soote season, that bud and bloom forth brings
>   B.B.F 48

Here we come a-piping, ANON
>   Here we come a-piping
>   COME 11

Last Snow, ANDREW YOUNG
  Although the snow still lingers
      P.W 258   YOU.P 81

Spring, THE BIBLE
  For lo, the winter is past, the rain is over and gone
      SONG OF SOLOMON ii 11   CH.GAR 81

Spring, GERARD MANLEY HOPKINS
  Nothing is so beautiful as spring
      OX.V.J IV 67

Spring, WILLIAM BLAKE
  Sound the flute !
      BLA.P 65   BLA.PENG 36   FAB.C.V 50

Spring, THOMAS NASHE
  Spring, the sweet spring, is the year's pleasant king
      COM 206   F.Y.D 20   KEY I 51
      MER 331   M.R.CHA 47   OX.P.C 102
      PAT 31   P.F.P I 117   TOM.T.G 55
      WHEEL III 67

The Spring, JOHN LYLY
  What bird so sings, yet so does wail?
      COME 15   THIS.W.D 70

Spring Comes, JOHN CLARE
  Spring comes and it is May. White as are sheets
      IRON I 97

Spring Quiet, CHRISTINA ROSSETTI
  Gone were but the winter
      KEY IV 110

Summer is y-cumin in, ANON
  Summer is y-cumin in
      CHER 48   COM 57   C.S.B 110 (P)
      KEY I 51   OX.E.V I

Weathers, THOMAS HARDY
This is the weather the cuckoo likes

A.D.L I 12	B.P IV 19	COME 10
ECHO I 90	FAB.C.V 59	HAR.PENG 163
HAR.SEL 32	MOD 3	MY 121
OX.P.C 96	P.F.P I 43	P.P.OVER 15
P.SING 21	P.TIME I 19	PUF.V 165
TOM.T.G 145	WEALTH 62	

When daisies pied, WILLIAM SHAKESPEARE
When daisies pied, and violets blue

LOVE'S LABOUR'S LOST V ii 902	C.S.B I 14 (P)
P.LIFE II 45	THIS.W.D 72

when faces called flowers, E. E. CUMMINGS
when faces called flowers float out of the ground

CUM.PENG 78

Written in March, WILLIAM WORDSWORTH
The cock is crowing

BL.J II 32	B.P IV 71	G.TR.P 270
KEY II 90	MER 362	M.R.FEEL 46
P.SING 22	THIS.W.D 103	TOM.T.G 37

SQUIRRELS

The Grey Squirrel, HUMBERT WOLFE
Like a small grey

PENG.AN 294

The Squirrel, IAN SERRAILLIER
Among the fox-red fallen leaves I surprised him, snap

OX.V.J IV 28   PUF.Q 175

The Squirrel, WILLIAM BROWNE
Then as a nimble squirrel from the wood

ECHO II 64

The Squirrel, CHRISTINA ROSSETTI
    Whisky, frisky
        TREE I 51

To a Squirrel at Kyle-na-no, W. B. YEATS
    Come play with me
        KEY II 40   OX.V.J I 51   THIS.W.D 45
        YEA.P 175

STAGS

A Runnable Stag, JOHN DAVIDSON
    When the pods went pop on the broom, green broom
        KEY III 88   PENG.AN 295   P.F.P III 85

STARS

Escape at Bedtime, R. L. STEVENSON
    The lights from the parlour and kitchen shone out
        A.D.L 268   G.TR.P 13   P.LIFE II 80
        P.REM 42

The Falling Star, SARA TEASDALE
    I saw a star slide down the sky
        OX.V.J III 72

On Making Certain Anything has Happened, ROBERT FROST
    I could be worse employed
        FRO.P 532   FRO.PENG 242

The Starlight Night, GERARD MANLEY HOPKINS
    Look at the stars! look, look up at the stars!
        AN.SPO II 99   DRUM 38

Star-Talk, ROBERT GRAVES
    Are you awake, Gemelli,
        A.D.L 16   AN.METH 93   KEY III 136

Waiting Both, THOMAS HARDY
    A star looks down on me
        HAR.PENG 187   OX.L.V 482

STATESMEN
See **Lincoln, Abraham**

STORMS
See also **Thunder & Lightning**

After the Storm, WILLIAM WORDSWORTH
>   There was a roaring on the wind all night
>> KEY III 130   OX.V.J IV 31

The Storm, EMILY DICKINSON
>   An awful tempest mashed the air
>> KEY III 130   OX.V.J III 74

SUBMARINES

Elegy for a Lost Submarine (1951), EWART MILNE
>   Would you talk to Davy Jones in his locker?
>> FLA 89

SUCCESS

What Then?, W. B. YEATS
>   His chosen comrades thought at school
>> SCH.M.V 197   YEA.P 347

SUMMER

The Ice Cart, W. W. GIBSON
>   Perched on my city office-stool
>> AN.METH 87   AN.SPO I 115   D.P.F.F 77
>> M.R.CHA 112   PEG II 2   P.F.P II 41
>> P.SING 73   SCH.M.V 59   WHEEL II 139

In the Mountains on a Summer Day, LI PO TRANS WALEY
>   Gently I stir a white feather fan
>> WAL.C.P 116

Raging Noon, JAMES THOMPSON
>   'Tis raging noon, and, vertical, the sun
>> KEY IV 145

Summer, CHRISTINA ROSSETTI
> Winter is cold-hearted
>> KEY I 77   OX.V.J III 28   P.W 215

SUN

Riddle on Moon and Sun, ANGLO-SAXON TRANS BONE
> I saw a creature sally with beauty
>> P.W 31

SUNRISE
See **Dawn**

SUPERNATURAL
See also **Charms & Spells: Fairies: Ghosts: Giants: Goblins: Magic: Mystery: Ogres: Robin Goodfellow: Trolls: Witches**

Lollocks, ROBERT GRAVES
> By sloth on sorrow fathered
>> CHER I55   DAY 38   GRA.P 190
>> GRA.PENG I40   KEY IV 60   PENG.C.V I32

SWANS

Either Bank, JOHN ROSCOE
> Look ! look ! swans by the dozen ! See how they glide
>> KEY IV 80

An Evening (Part), WILLIAM WORDSWORTH
> He swells his lifted chest, and backward flings
>> PENG.AN 300

The Silver Swan, ANON
> The silver swan which living had no note
>> KEY IV 80

The Swans, ANDREW YOUNG
> How lovely are these swans
>> WEALTH 70   YOU.P 83

The Wild Swans at Coole, W. B. YEATS
    The trees are in their autumn beauty
        FLA 30   WEALTH 219   YEA.P 147

TALES, CAUTIONARY

The Boy Who Laughed at Santa Claus, OGDEN NASH
    In Baltimore there lived a boy
        KEY III 85

Greedy Richard, JANE TAYLOR
    I think I want some pies this morning
        PUF.V 136

TALES, CAUTIONARY (BELLOC)

See also BEL.PUF

George, H. BELLOC
    When George's Grandmamma was told
        M.M.A 8

Henry King, H. BELLOC
    The chief defect of Henry King
        BEL.PUF 22   PEG I 9   PENG.COM 32
        P.LIFE II 16

Jim, H. BELLOC
    There was a boy whose name was Jim
        A.D.L 239   BEL.PUF 15   CHER 22
        ECHO I 72   EX.T.CH 89   FAB.N.V 161
        MER 284   PEG I 10   SPIR 6

Matilda, H. BELLOC
    Matilda told such dreadful lies
        BEL.PUF 26   D.P.JOU 34   EX.T.TRO 59
        FAB.C.V 96   M.R.ON 30   OX.P.C 30
        PEG I 12   PENG.COM 32   P.LIFE IV 90
        PUF.V 152   V.F 18   WHEEL I 29

TALES, TALL

TEENAGERS

THISTLES

Thistledown, ANDREW YOUNG
> Silver against blue sky
>> YOU.P 90

Thistles, TED HUGHES
> Against the rubber tongues of cows
> and the hoeing hands of men
>> THEME 57

THRUSHES

The Darkling Thrush, THOMAS HARDY
> I leant upon a coppice gate
>> HAR.PENG 51   HAR.SEL I   R.R 89

The Missel-Thrush, ANDREW YOUNG
> That missel-thrush
>> YOU.P 148

The Missel Thrush, WALTER DE LA MARE
> When from the brittle ice the fields
>> B.B.F 116   IRON I 123

Stormcock in Elder, RUTH PITTER
> In my dark hermitage, aloof
>> OX.V.J IV 35

The Thrush's Nest, JOHN CLARE
> Within a thick and spreading hawthorn bush
>> B.B.F 34   M.R.HAND 57   MY 118
>> P.F.P I 121

THUNDER & LIGHTNING

Beware, ANON
> Beware of an oak
>> KEY III 17

TIDES

TIGERS

The Tyger, WILLIAM BLAKE

Tyger, tyger, burning bright

TIGHTROPES

Blondin, WALTER DE LA MARE

With clinging, dainty, cat-like tread

TIME

Candles, C. P. CAVAFY

The days of our future stand before us

Cities and Thrones and Powers, RUDYARD KIPLING

Cities and thrones and powers

Lines on a Clock in Chester Cathedral, HENRY TWELLS

When, as a child, I laughed and wept

Sic Vita, HENRY KING

Like to the falling of a star

Sonnet XLIV, WILLIAM SHAKESPEARE

When I have seen by Time's fell hand defaced

Written on the Night before his Execution, SIR WALTER RALEGH
 Even such is Time, which takes in trust
   CHER 381   OX.V.J IV 91 R.R 100
   WEALTH 286

TIMES PAST

In the British Museum, THOMAS HARDY
 What do you see in that time-touched stone?
   HAR.PENG 118 HAR.SEL 63

On Wenlock Edge, A. E. HOUSMAN
 On Wenlock Edge the wood's in trouble
   HOU.P 48 P.P.FAL 73

Then, WALTER DE LA MARE
 Twenty, forty, sixty, eighty
   COM 107   DE LA M.P II 135 EX.T.H 15
   OX.V.J II 9 P.LIFE I 69 P.P.FACT 80

TITMICE

Titmouse, WALTER DE LA MARE
 If you would happy company win
   DE LA M.CH 42

TOADS

The Death of a Toad, RICHARD WILBUR
 A toad the power mower caught
   PENG.M.A.V 301

The Toad, E. L. M. KING
 As I was running down the road
   TREE III 23

TOASTS

Down among the Dead Men, ANON
 Here's a health to the Queen and a lasting peace
   OX.S.M.S III 13 (M)

Old Toast, ANON
    Happy have we met
        WEALTH I

TOOTHACHE

A Charm against the Toothache, JOHN HEATH-STUBBS
    Venerable Mother Toothache
        DAWN 53   MY 159   PENG.C.V 307

TORTOISES

Baby Tortoise, D. H. LAWRENCE
    You know what it is to be born alone
        FLA 47   LAW.PENG 101   UNDER 117
Meditations of a Tortoise, E. V. RIEU
    One cannot have enough
        PUF.Q 130
    So far as I can see
        PUF.Q 123
    The world is very flat
        PUF.Q 137

TOWNS
See **Cities & Towns**

TRACTORS

Cynddylan on a Tractor, R. S. THOMAS
    Ah! you should see Cynddylan on a Tractor
        DAWN 78   HAP 26   HERE 18
        WHEEL IV 188
New Farm Tractor, CARL SANDBURG
    Snub nose, the guts of twenty mules are in your cylinders
        and transmission
        PEG III 51

TRADE UNIONS
My Master and I, ANON
>   Says the master to me, 'Is it true? I am told'
>>   C.MUSE 175

TRADES & PROFESSIONS
See also **Actors: Bird Catchers: Blacksmiths** See also **Farriers: Bricklayers: Bus Drivers: Butchers: Carters: Charcoal Burners: Chimney Sweeps: Dustmen: Engine Drivers & Firemen: Engineers: Explorers: Farmers: Farm Workers: Farriers: Ferrymen: Financiers: Firemen** See **Engine Drivers: Firemen (Fire-Fighting): Fishermen: Foresters: Gamekeepers: Gardeners: Gipsies: Hermits: Highwaymen: Hoboes** See **Tramps: Housewives: Knife Grinders: Loggers: Miners: Mole Catchers: Painters: Pedlars: Pipers: Pirates: Poachers: Poets: Rag & Bone Men: Sailors: Scientists: Shoemakers: Smugglers: Soldiers: Tramps & Hoboes: Watermen** See **Ferrymen: Woodmen** See also **Foresters**

Cherry Stones, A. A. MILNE
>   Tinker, Tailor
>>   (for original, see OX.N.R 110)
>>>   MIL.N.S 19

Street Songs, See OX.N.R 72–3

TRAFALGAR
The Night of Trafalgar, THOMAS HARDY
>   In the wild October night-time,
>>   when the wind raved round the land

A.D.L 251	AN.SPO I 118	CHER 340
COME 177	ECHO I 45	FAB.C.V 258
MOD 8	P. TONG 66	

Victory (c. 1805), ANON
>   I am a youthful lady, my troubles they are great
>>   C.MUSE 131

TRAINS

See also **Accidents (on the Railway): Engine Drivers: U.S.A.: Railroads**

See PEG II 78–87

The Bridge, J. REDWOOD ANDERSON
    Here, with one leap
        KEY IV 50   SPIR 65

The Bridge (Part), J. REDWOOD ANDERSON
    . . . Out of the silence grows
        P.LIFE IV 38   P.P.BEL I 57

Diesel Train, A. D. G. HANSON
    Free from the hiss of pressurised steam
        KEY III 34

The Egg and the Machine, ROBERT FROST
    He gave the solid rail a hateful kick
        FRO.P 349   FRO.PENG 171   KEY IV 52

The Engine Driver, CLIVE SANSOM
    The train goes running along the line
        BL.J I 49

The Express, STEPHEN SPENDER
    After the first powerful plain manifesto

A.D.L 147	ALB I 161	COM 176
DAY 11	D.P.F.F 125	MOD 217
PAT 156	PEG IV 98	P.F.P II 153
SCH.M.V I 57		

The Figure in the Doorway, ROBERT FROST
    The grade surmounted we were riding high
        FRO.P 378   FRO.PENG 187

From a Railway Carriage, R. L. STEVENSON
    Faster than fairies, faster than witches

A.D.L 149	AN.SPO I 152	DRUM 62
EX.T.TRO 32	MER 185	M.R.FEEL 65
OX.V.J II 48	P.LIFE II 49	

I like to see it lap the miles, EMILY DICKINSON
　　I like to see it lap the miles
　　　　　BL.J III 64　　　　　PEG II 83　　　　　PENG.M.A.V 34
　　　　　R.R 70

Limited, CARL SANDBURG
　　I am riding on a limited express,
　　　　one of the crack trains of the nation
　　　　　IRON II 88　　　　PENG.M.A.V 63

Morning Express, S. SASSOON
　　Along the wind-swept platform, pinched and white
　　　　　P.SING 134　　　　R.R 68

Night Mail, W. H. AUDEN
　　This is the night mail crossing the border
　　　　　A.D.L 147　　　　　B.P IV 92　　　　　CHER 407
　　　　　D.P.ROAD 90　　　　EX.T.CH 160　　　　KEY IV 120
　　　　　M.R.ON 22　　　　　OX.V.J III 23　　　　PEG II 86
　　　　　P.F.P II 154　　　　P.LIFE IV 40　　　　P.REM 52
　　　　　SPIR 60　　　　　　WEALTH 280　　　　WHEEL II 157

Puffing Billy, C. HASSALL
　　Oh the grand approach at Euston
　　　　　KEY II 22

Sic Transit, J. K. R. THORNE
　　In the vast and gloomy precincts of the ancient engine-shed
　　　　　KEY II 27

Skimbleshanks the Railway Cat, T. S. ELIOT
　　There's a whisper down the line at 11.39
　　　　　CH.GAR 52　　　　　D.P.WAY 30　　　　EL.O.P 40
　　　　　EX.T.CH 156　　　　FAB.C.V 285　　　　M.R.ON 51
　　　　　PENG.M.C 164　　　　P.P.OVER 74　　　　V.F 58
　　　　　WHEEL I 149

Song of a Train, JOHN DAVIDSON
　　A monster taught
　　　　　AN.SPO I 108

TRAINS (UNDERGROUND)

TRAMPS & HOBOES

TRANSPORT
See **Accidents: Aeroplanes: Boats: Bus Drivers: Engine Drivers: Ships: Trains**

TRANSPORTATION
Botany Bay, ANON
Come all you men of learning
M.R.CHA 98

Van Dieman's Land, ANON
Come all you gallant poachers, that ramble void of care
BAL 708   C.MUSE 236   FAB.BAL 225
KEY II 13

TRAPEZES
The Man on the Flying Trapeze, ANON
O the girl that I loved she was handsome
M.M.A 92

TRAVEL
See **Exploring: Journeys: Transport**

TREACHERY
The Castle, EDWIN MUIR
All through that summer at ease we lay
M.CENT 34   TW.N 18   UNDER 76

TREES
See also **Apple Trees: Aspens: Beeches: Birches: Cherry Trees: Holly: Oaks: Pines: Plane Trees: Poplars: Woods**

Beware, ANON
Beware of an oak
KEY III 17

A Fallen Tree, P. FERNANDO
> Suddenly in a wood, beyond all lumber lore and reason
>> KEY IV 22

The Hill Pines, ROBERT BRIDGES
> The hill pines were sighing
>> KEY IV 23

Pruning Trees, CHINESE TRANS WALEY
> Trees growing—right in front of my window
>> WAL.C.P 171

Throwing a Tree: New Forest, THOMAS HARDY
> The two executioners stalk along over the knolls
>> FLA 26   HAR.PENG 204   IRON II 52
>> KEY IV 24

The Tree in the Wood, ANON·
> All in the Wood there was a Tree
>> KEY II 79

Trees, WALTER DE LA MARE
> Of all the trees in England
>> DE LA M.CH 38   DE LA M.P II 231   OX.V.J IV 56
>> TREE IV 76

A Tree Song, RUDYARD KIPLING
> Of all the trees that grow so fair
>> KIP.INC 489

TROLLS

Troll sat alone, J. J. R. TOLKIEN
> Troll sat alone on his seat of stone
>> KEY IV 42

TURPIN, DICK

My Bonny Black Bess, ANON
> Dick Turpin bold! Dick, hie away
>> C.MUSE 233

TURTLES

The Little Turtle, VACHEL LINDSAY
    There was a little turtle
        BL.J II 38   LIN.P 67

Tony the Turtle, E. V. RIEU
    Tony was a turtle
        D.P.JOU 37   EX.T.TRO 17   FAB.N.V 85
        P.LIFE III 75   PUF.Q 124

UNCLES

My Uncle Dan, TED HUGHES
    My Uncle Dan's an inventor, you may think that's very fine
        HU.MEET 33   TREE IV 98

UNITED STATES OF AMERICA
See also **Buffaloes: Cowboys: Freedom Songs: Indians, Red**

American Names, S. V. BENÉT
    I have fallen in love with American names
        PEG V 66   PENG.M.A.V 194

In praise of Johnny Appleseed, VACHEL LINDSAY
    In the days of President Washington
        LIN.P 82

UNITED STATES OF AMERICA: CIVIL WAR
See also **Lincoln, Abraham**

Barbara Frietchie, J. G. WHITTIER
    Up from the meadows rich with corn
        EX.T.CH 106   G.TR.P 190   M.R ON 96
        PEG II 47

Battle Hymn of the Republic, JULIA WARD HOWE
    Mine eyes have seen the glory of the coming of the Lord
        COME I 70   FIRE.F.S 220 (P)   G.TR.P 311

The Rebel, INNES RANDOLPH
  Oh, I'm a good old rebel, that's what I am
   OX.L.V 436

The Rebel Soldier, ANON
  One morning, one morning, one morning in May
   OX.L.V 436   P.TONG 108   TREE III 53

Yellow Rose of Texas, ANON
  There's a yellow rose in Texas
   S.T.S II 60 (G,P)

UNITED STATES OF AMERICA: DUST BOWLS

So long, WOODY GUTHRIE
  I'll sing you a song and I'll sing it again
   A.F.B 92 (G)   PENG.A.F.S 244 (G,P)

UNITED STATES OF AMERICA: FARMING

The Boll Weevil, ANON
  O have you heard de lates'
   B.L.A.F.S 236 (G,P) F.S.N.A 535 (G,B,P)
   PENG.A.F.S 146 (G,P)

The Farmer is the Man, ANON
  When the farmer comes to town
   A.F.B 57 (G)   F.S.N.A 132 (G,B)

When I first came to this land, ANON
  When I first came to this land
   A.F.B 13 (G)   S.T.S II 6 (G,P)

UNITED STATES OF AMERICA: PIONEERS & THE WEST

The Ballad of William Sycamore, S. V. BENÉT
  My father, he was a mountaineer
   M.R.CHA 117   PEG III 79   SPIR 39

The Ox-Tamer, WALT WHITMAN
    In a far away northern county
        KEY IV 150

The Stage Driver's Story, BRET HARTE
    It was the stage driver's story
        KEY III 124

Starving to death on a Government Claim, ANON
    My name is Tom Hight, an old bachelor I am
        B.L.A.F.S 238 (G,P)   WHEEL IV 127

Sweet Betsy from Pike, ANON
    Did you ever hear tell of sweet Betsy from Pike?
        BAL 750   B.L.A.F.S 176 (G,P)   FAB.BAL 239
        FIRE.F.S 62 (P)   F.S.N.A 335 (G,B)   IVES 234 (G,P)
        PENG.A.F.S 170 (G,P)

Western Wagons, S. V. BENÉT
    They went with axe and rifle when the trail was still to blaze
        PEG II 71

UNITED STATES OF AMERICA: RAILROADS

Casey Jones, ANON
    Come all you rounders that want to hear
        B.L.A.F.S 266 (G,P)   D.P.WAY 34   EX.T.CH 164
        FIRE.F.S 142 (P)   F.S.N.A 564 (G,B)   IRON II 77
        KEY I 84   M.M.A 23   M.R.ON 20
        OX.L.V 453   OX.P.C 76   OX.V.J IV 25
        PEG II 78   P.F.P I 156   P.P.WIDE 68
        P.TONG 17   SPIR 58   S.T.S I 12 (G)
    On a Sunday morning it begins to rain
        B.L.A.F.S 264 (G,P)
    Some folks say Casey Jones can't run
        PENG.A.F.S 216 (G,P)

Drill, ye Tarriers, Drill, ANON
  Ev'ry morning at seven o'clock
    FIRE.F.S 138 (P)   F.S.N.A 417 (G,B)   S.T.S II 26 (G,P)

John Henry, ANON
  John Henry was a little boy
    A.F.B 82 (G)   BAL 756   B.L.A.F.S 258 (G,P)
    FAB.BAL 243   F.S.N.A 562 (G,B)   IRON II 95
    OX.L.V 442   PEG II 76
    PENG.A.F.S 150 (G,P)
  John Henry said to his captain
    FIRE.F.S 170 (P)
  Well, it's honey an' it's darlin' when I'm here
    F.S.N.A 560 (G,B)

Paddy works on the Erie/Railway, ANON
  In eighteen hundred and forty-one/eighty-one
    FIRE.F.S 150 (P)   KEY I 60
    PENG.A.F.S 216 (G,P)

To a Locomotive in Winter, WALT WHITMAN
  Thee for my recitative
    PEG IV 47

What the Engines said (Opening of the Pacific Railroad),
  BRET HARTE
  What was it the engines said
    KEY IV 122

UNITED STATES OF AMERICA: SLAVERY
See also **Slave Trade**

All the Pretty Little Horses, ANON
  Hush-you-bye (OR Hush-a-bye)
    B.L.A.F.S 14 (G,P)   C.S.B 90 (P)   OX.L.V 435
    PENG.A.F.S 96 (G,P)

Black Sheep, ANON
  Black sheep, black sheep
    F.S.N.A 503 (G,B)

The Blue-Tail Fly, ANON
  When I was young I used to wait
        A.F.B 12 (G)   F.S.N.A 505 (G,B)   IVES 206 (G,P)
        PENG A.F.S 104 (G,P) R.R 176   S.N.W 42 (G,P)

The Slave's Dream, H. W. LONGFELLOW
  Beside the ungathered rice he lay
        WEALTH 36

UNITED STATES OF AMERICA: WAR OF INDEPENDENCE

If, Yankees, you would have a song, R. SHUCKBURGH
  If, Yankees, you would have a song
        IVES 72 (G,P)

Johnny has gone for a soldier, ANON
  O Johnny dear has gone away
        F.S.N.A 47 (G,B,P)
  There I sit on Butternut Hill
        B.L.A.F.S 117 (G,P)   FIRE.F.S 69 (P)   IVES 98 (G,P)
        S.N.W 23 (G,P)

Paul Revere's Ride, H. W. LONGFELLOW
  Listen my children and you shall hear
        D.P.WAY 87   EX.T.CH 98   G.TR.P 184
        SPIR 162

The Star-Spangled Banner, F. SCOTT KEY
  Oh say, can you see, by the dawn's early light
        FIRE.F.S 184 (P)

Yankee Doodle, ANON
  Yankee Doodle went to town
        PENG.A.F.S 30 (G,P)

VEGETABLES
See **Celery: Parsnip**

  K

VICTORIA

Queen Victoria (1837), ANON
> Welcome now, VICTORIA!
>> C.MUSE 139

VIKINGS

Harp Song of the Dane Women, RUDYARD KIPLING
> What is a woman that you forsake her
>> KIP.INC 515   PEG IV 103   PENG.E.V 402
>> P.TIME 18   R.R 38   SCH.M.V 81

VILLAGES

Our Village—by a Villager, THOMAS HOOD
> Our village, that's to say not Miss Mitford's village
>   but our village of Bullock Smithy
>> R.R 79

VIOLINS

At the Railway Station, Upwey, THOMAS HARDY
> There is not much that I can do
>> KEY III 36

Fiddle, ANON
> And Tommy had a fiddle too
>> KEY III 146

The Fiddler of Dooney, W. B. YEATS
> When I play on my fiddle in Dooney
>> A.D.L 127   AN.SPO I 166   EX.T.CH I 54
>> FAB.C.V 41   M.R.CHA 10   OX.V.J II 26
>> PEG II 99   P.LIFE III 42   YEA.P 82

The Penny Fiddle, ROBERT GRAVES
> Yesterday I bought a penny fiddle
>> GRA.FID 8

WALKING

The End of the Road, H. BELLOC
    In these boots and with this staff
        P.F.P I 12   PUF.V 179

WAR
See also **Battles: Blitz: Nuclear War: Refugees: Sea Battles: Soldiers**

The Ash and the Oak, LOUIS SIMPSON
    When men discovered freedom first
        PENG.C.A.P 97

Conquerors, HENRY TREECE
    By sundown we came to a hidden village
        HERE 41   UNDER 85

A Day with the Foreign Legion, REED WHITMORE
    On one of those days with the Legion
        PENG.C.A.P 51

The Drum, JOHN SCOTT
    I hate that drum's discordant sound
        KEY III 71   PEG II 45

A Drumlin Woodchuck, ROBERT FROST
    One thing has a shelving bank
        FRO.P 365   FRO.PENG 182   FRO.YOU 50

The Horses, EDWIN MUIR
    Barely a twelvemonth after
        R.R 185   THEME I 54

In Time of the Breaking of Nations, THOMAS HARDY
    Only a man harrowing clods
        AN.METH 104   HAR.PENG I 59   HAR.SEL 65

Johnny, I hardly knew ye, ANON
    While going along the road to sweet Athy
        ECHO III I 55   FAB.BAL 212   OX.L.V 316

The Man he Killed, THOMAS HARDY
    Had he and I but met
        HAR.PENG 82   KEY IV 17

Nightmare, W. KIRKCONNELL
    I saw my dream grow darker yet
        KEY IV 148

On Appleton House (Part), ANDREW MARVELL
    See how the flowers, as at parade
        R.R 45

The Other Time, PETER APPLETON
    He killed a man
        KEY IV 18

The Performance, JAMES DICKEY
    The last time I saw Donald Armstrong
        PENG.C.A.P 77

Protest in the Sixth Year of Ch'ien Fu, CHINESE TRANS WALEY
    The hills and rivers of the lowland country
        KEY III 68   M.P.W 95   WAL.C.P 193

This Excellent Machine, JOHN LEHMANN
    This excellent machine is neatly planned
        THEME 151

The White Horse, TU FU TRANS REWI ALLEY
    Out of the Northeast
        CHER 343

WAR: FALSE PATRIOTISM

Call, D. B. WYNDHAM LEWIS
    He cried: 'Let England to herself be true!'
        PENG.M.C 221

Memorial Tablet, S. SASSOON
    Squire nagged and bullied till I went to fight
        R.R 50

next to of course God america i, E. E. CUMMINGS
next to of course God america i

WAR: PRIVATE SOLDIERS

Snapshot of Nairobi, ROY CAMPBELL
With orange-peel the streets are strewn

WARS: CRIMEAN

The Charge of the Light Brigade, LORD TENNYSON
Half a league, half a league

WARS: BOER

Drummer Hodge, THOMAS HARDY
They throw in Drummer Hodge to rest

The Man he Killed, THOMAS HARDY
Had he and I but met

WARS: 1914–18 (GENERAL)

All the Hills and Vales along, CHARLES SORLEY
All the hills and vales along

Anthem for Doomed Youth, WILFRED OWEN
What passing bells for those who die as cattle?

Channel Firing, THOMAS HARDY
    That night your great guns, unawares
        FLA 22   HAR.PENG 85   HAR.SEL 61

The General, S. SASSOON
    'Good morning! good morning!' the General said
        OX.L.V 524   PEG IV 93

Inspection, WILFRED OWEN
    'You! What d'you mean by this?' I rapped
        IRON II 71   OWEN.P 79

Into Battle (1915), JULIAN GRENFELL
    The naked earth is warm with spring
        D.P.F.F 92   P.TIME 94

Lost in France, ERNEST RHYS
    He had the ploughman's strength
        ALB I 135   PEG IV 87   P.TIME 95

To Any Dead Officer, S. SASSOON
    Well, how are things in Heaven? I wish you'd say
        FLA 54

WARS: 1914–18 (AIR)

An Irish Airman Foresees his Death, W. B. YEATS
    I know that I shall meet my fate
        FAB.C.V 270   FAB.N.V 70   D.P.F.F 88
        R.R 48   YEA.P 152

When the Plane Dived, WILFRID GIBSON
    When the plane dived and the machine-gun spattered
        PEG IV 94

WARS: 1914–18 (GAS)

Dulce et Decorum est, WILFRED OWEN
    Bent double, like old beggars under sacks
        M.P.W 72   OWEN.P 55   PEG IV 94
        R.R 47   THEME 94   WHEEL III 163

WARS: 1914–18 (SEA)

Mine Sweepers, RUDYARD KIPLING
>   Dawn off the Foreland—the young flood making
>>   KIP.INC 612

Mine-Sweeping Trawlers, E. HILTON YOUNG
>   Not ours the fighter's glow
>>   PEG II 44

My Boy Jack, RUDYARD KIPLING
>   Have you news of my boy Jack?
>>   KIP.INC 213

When the Plane Dived, WILFRID GIBSON
>   When the plane dived and the machine-gun spattered
>>   PEG IV 94

WARS: 1914–18 (TRENCHES)

Counter-attack, S. SASSOON
>   We'd gained our first objective hours before
>>   FLA 52

Exposure, WILFRED OWEN
>   Our brains ache in the merciless iced east winds that knive us
>>   EV.M 75   FAB.M.V 175   OWEN.P 48
>>   PENG.C.V 119

WARS: 1939–45 (AIR)

The Death of the Ball Turret Gunner, RANDALL JARELL
>   From my mother's sleep I fell into the State
>>   PENG.M.A.V 269

For Johnny, JOHN PUDNEY
>   Do not despair
>>   DAY 75   WEALTH 49   WHEEL IV 183

Hiroshima, A SCHOOLCHILD
>   Noon, and hazy heat
>>   EV.M 77   WHEEL IV 210

WARS: 1939–45 (CHURCHILL)

WARS: 1939–45 (PROPAGANDA)

WARS: 1939–45 (SEA)

The 'Jervis Bay', MICHAEL THWAITES
  But the days and the weeks and the months ran on,
    with little to see or show
      SPIR 171

WARS: 1939–45 (TRAINING)

Lessons of the War, HENRY REED
  Today we have naming of parts. Yesterday
      PENG.C.V 288   R.R 53   SPIR 90
      WEALTH 254   WHEEL IV 184

WARS: CYPRUS

The Song of the Dead Soldier, CHRISTOPHER LOGUE
  For seven years at school I named
      WHEEL IV 195

WASHING (CLOTHES)

Dashing away with the Smoothing-Iron, ANON
  'Twas on a Monday morning
      TREE III 28

The Shepherd's Hut, ANDREW YOUNG
  The smear of blue peat smoke
      BL.J IV 27   YOU.P 197

Washdays, ANON
  They that wash on Monday
      BL.J III 1

WATERFALLS

The Cataract of Lodore, ROBERT SOUTHEY
  How does the water
      D.P.JOU 43   KEY III 28

WATERMEN
See **Ferrymen**

WAVES

The Horses of the Sea, CHRISTINA ROSSETTI
    The horses of the sea
        BL.J I 55   OX.V.J II 79   TREE II 27

Waves, ELEANOR FARJEON
    There are big waves and little waves
        BL.J I 56

WEATHER
See also **Clouds: Fog: Frost & Ice: Months: Rain: Seasons: Snow: Thaw: Thunder: Wind**

Weather Lore: see FAB.N.V 230

Weather Wise: see OX.N.R 117–8

Signs of Rain, EDWARD JENNER
    The hollow winds begin to blow
        M.R.CHA 40

Weather Ear, NORMAN NICHOLSON
    Lying in bed in the dark, I hear the bray
        DAWN 105

Weathers, THOMAS HARDY
    This is the weather the cuckoo likes
        A.D.L 112   B.P IV 19   COME 10
        ECHO I 90   FAB.C.V 59   HAR.PENG 163
        HAR.SEL 32   MOD 3   MY 121
        OX.P.C 96   P.F.P I 43   P.P.OVER 15
        P.SING 21   P.TIME 119   PUF.V 165
        TOM.T.G 145   WEALTH 62

WHALES

The Progress of the Soul (Part), JOHN DONNE
  At every stroke his brazen finnes do take
    A.A 72   CHER 210   DRUM 74
    KEY IV 111   P.TONG II 5
The Whale, ANON
  To explain the nature of fishes in craft of verse
    P.W 32

WHALING

The Boston Come-All-Ye, ANON
Blow, Ye winds in the Morning, ANON
  'Tis advertised in Boston, New York and Buffalo
    B.L.A.F.S 144 (G,P) IVES 146 (G,P)   PENG.A.F.S 36 (G,P)
The Greenland Whale Fishery, ANON
The Whale, ANON
  In seventeen hundred and ninety-four
    P.F.P I 152   IVES 148 (G,P)
  'Twas eighteen hundred and twenty
    F.S.N.A 61 (G,B)   WHEEL II 83
  'Twas in the year of forty-nine
    CHER 208   P.TONG 70
  'Twas in eighteen hundred and fifty-three
    TREE III 100
  We can no longer stay on shore
    BAL 707

WIND

And it was windy weather, JAMES STEPHENS
  Now the winds are riding by
    EX.T.CH 30   OX.V.J III 73
Arthur O'Bower has broken his band, ANON
  Arthur O'Bower has broken his band
    CHER 389   FAB.C.V 62

WINTER
See also **Frost & Ice: Months: Seasons: Snow: Snowflakes: Weather**

Alone, WALTER DE LA MARE
 The abode of the nightingale is bare
  WHEEL IV 147

The Backs in February, JOHN PRESS
 Winter's keen blade has stripped
  PEG IV 48

A Carol, RUDYARD KIPLING
 Our Lord who did the Ox command
  KIP.INC 501

The Darkling Thrush, THOMAS HARDY
 I leant upon a coppice gate
  HAR.PENG 51   HAR.SEL I   R.R 89

Hot Cake, SHU HSI TRANS WALEY
 Winter has come; fierce is the cold
  A.D.L 101   IRON II 68   WAL.C.P 86

To Winter, WILLIAM BLAKE
 Oh winter, bar thine adamantine door
  BLA.P 5   R.R 94

When icicles hang by the wall, WILLIAM SHAKESPEARE
 When icicles hang by the wall

LOVE'S LABOUR'S LOST V ii 920		A.A 46
B.B.F 109	CHER 392	CH.GAR 20
COM 76	COME 246	D.P.JOU 106
ECHO I 96	FAB.C.V 56	F.Y.D 57
IRON I 50	KEY I 75	MER 348
M.R.HAND 6	OX.P.C 98	OX.V.J II 59
PAT 21	P.F.P I 44	P.LIFE II·58
P.P.TALK 78	PUF.V 128	THIS.W.D 72

Winter, WALTER DE LA MARE
　　Clouded with snow
　　　　DE LA M.P I 128　　　WHEEL I 135

Winter, HENRY TREECE
　　Do you know the snow?
　　　　MOD 238

Winter, LORD TENNYSON
　　The frost is here
　　　　BL.J IV 16　　　　　TREE III 40

Winter, WALTER DE LA MARE
　　Green mistletoe
　　　　CHER 394　　　　　DE LA M.CH 51　　　DE LA M.P I 96

Winter, R. L. STEVENSON
　　In rigorous hours, when down the iron lane
　　　　PEG I 109　　　　WEALTH 63

A Winter Night, EDWARD FITZGERALD
　　'Tis a dull sight
　　　　PEG I 113

Winter's Beauty, W. H. DAVIES
　　Is it not fine to walk in spring
　　　　TREE IV 23

The Words of Finn, ANON
　　My words for you
　　　　CHER 389

WISDOM

But where shall wisdom be found?, THE BIBLE
　　　　JOB XXVIII 12–28

Happy is the man that findeth wisdom, THE BIBLE
　　　　PROVERBS iii 13–8　　AN.SPO II 45

WITCHES
See also **Charms & Spells**

The Witch, MARY COLERIDGE
    I have walked a great while over the snow
        OX.V.J III 53

WOLVES

Hunting Song of the Seeonee Pack, RUDYARD KIPLING
    As the dawn was breaking the sambhur belled
        KIP.INC 648

The Supper, WALTER DE LA MARE
    A wolf he pricks with eyes of fire
        DE LA M.CH 84

WOODLARKS

The Woodlark, GERARD MANLEY HOPKINS
    Teevo cheevo cheevio chee
        KEY I 53

WOODMEN
See also **Foresters**

Throwing a Tree in the New Forest, THOMAS HARDY
    The two executioners stalk along over the knolls
        FLA 26   HAR.PENG 204   IRON II 52
        KEY IV 24

WOODPECKERS

The Woodpecker, ANDREW MARVELL
    He walks still upright from the root
        B.B.F 93   CHER 96

WOODS
See also **Trees**

An English Wood, ROBERT GRAVES
    This valley wood is pledged
        GRA.P 29   GRA.PENG 34   PEG V 35

Yak, WILLIAM JAY SMITH
> The long-haired yak has long black hair
>> G.TR.P 55

ZODIAC

The Signs of the Zodiac, ANON
> The Ram, the Bull, the Heavenly Twins
>> Y.B.S ix

ZOO

The Bear, FREDERICK BROWN
> His sullen, shaggy-rimmed eyes followed my every move
>> EV.M 21

Exile, V. SHEARD
> Ben-Arabie was the camel
>> ALB I 157

Our Visit to the Zoo, JESSIE POPE
> When we went to the Zoo
>> B.P II 34   P.P.BELL 14

The Water Zoo, E. V. KNOX
> Today I have seen all I wish
>> PEG IV 18

The Zoo in the City, SARA VAN A. ALLEN
> Enclose the lacquered, coiling snake
>> P.SING 63

Books to which reference is made

Explanation of symbols used for books

The symbol used for a book of poems by a single author begins with the first three letters of the poet's name, and P indicates that it is a collected edition: e.g. FRO.P, *Collected Poems of Robert Frost*; HAR.PENG the Penguin *Selection of Hardy's Poems*: REE.W.M, James Reeves' *Wandering Moon*.

Anthologies are coded by title: e.g. HAP, *Happenings*; HERE, *Here Today*. When there is a series of numbered volumes, graded for classroom use, the volumes are indicated by Roman figures, the pages by Arabic numbers: e.g. PEG V 21 is *Pegasus*, volume V, page 21. When the series is not numbered on the cover, an indication of the main title is given, followed by a different symbol for each volume: EX.T.CH and EX.T.H belong to the Exploring Poetry series, and are *Treasure Chest and Treasure Hunt*. The letters F.S appear in all the symbols for collections of folk-songs, except A.F.B, *American Favorite Ballads* and S.N.W., *Songs of the New World*.

Such indications as FAB, Faber; PENG, Penguin; PUF, Puffin and OX, Oxford are easily recognizable.

If the poem is accompanied by music, a letter follows the page number: (M) for melody only, (G) and (B) for guitar and banjo chords respectively, (R) for recorder descant with melody, and (P) for piano accompaniment.

A.A

Animals All, ed. A. BODY
Cambridge University Press 1940

> Poems and prose extracts about animals, chosen to appeal to children. Also short bibliography of further poems and stories about animals.

A.B.L.P

Albatross Book of Longer Poems, ed. EDWIN MORGAN
Collins London 1963

> Ninety (adult and mostly difficult) poems from Chaucer and Milton to Logue and Ginsberg. For older, more academic children. All the poems require sustained attention. Useful notes.

A.D.L

All Day Long, comp. PAMELA WHITLOCK
Oxford 1954, 2nd imp. 1957

> Unusual poems, often rather difficult, arranged by subject. A book for the teacher to use.

A.F.B

American Favorite Ballads as sung by PETE SEEGER
Oak Publications New York 1961

> More than eighty popular songs and ballads of all kinds; tunes, lyrics and guitar chords. Brief introduction to each song, explaining provenance. Admirable for class singing.

ALB

The Albemarle Book of Modern Verse for Schools I, II, ed. F. E. S. FINN
Murray London 1962

> Recent poems both grave and gay, usually sophisticated, chosen for their connection with daily life. Might start discussions in upper forms.

AN.E.P

A Background Anthology of English Poetry, ed. D. PROTHERO and J. W. ROCHE
Arnold London 1953

> A rather academic selection of poems by important poets from Chaucer to the present day.

AN.JEN
An Anthology of Modern Verse 1940-60, chosen E. JENNINGS
Methuen London 1961

> Poems too complicated for children's own reading, but a keen teacher could use this book to lead older children to modern poetry.

AN.METH
An Anthology of Modern Verse, ed. A. METHUEN
Methuen London 1921, 42nd edn. 1946

> Mainly Georgian poetry, much of which still appeals to adolescents.

AN.SPO
An Anthology of Spoken Verse and Prose I, II, selected G. JOHNSON, J. BYRNE and C. BURNISTON
Oxford University Press 1957

> A wide selection, including contemporary work, specially chosen for choral speaking by schoolchildren, with suggested arrangements.

AN.WAI
Anthology of Modern Poetry, ed. JOHN WAIN
Hutchinson Educational 1963

> Rather difficult poems (1870-1960) grouped by subject, for top forms. Introduction and notes.

AUD.PENG
W. H. AUDEN
Penguin London 1958

> The author's own selection of poems written from 1927 to 1954, arranged in more or less chronological order. Older children enjoy Auden's ballads and folk-songs.

BAL
The Ballad Book, ed. MACEDWARD LEACH
A. S. Barnes & Co. New York, Thomas Yoseloff London 1955

> Comprehensive collection of 370 English, Scottish and

American ballads, with notes, glossary, bibliography and discography. Very good source book for school and class libraries.

B.B.F

Birds, Beasts and Fishes, ed. R. MANNING-SANDERS
Oxford University Press 1962
One of the best anthologies of animal poetry; an amazing variety, including Anglo-Saxon riddles and Dunbar, passages from Isaiah and Whitman, and nonsense poems.

BEL.PUF

Selected Cautionary Verses, by H. BELLOC
Puffin rev. edn. 1964
The immortal Jim, Matilda and many others of Belloc's children, beasts and peers. A most enjoyable selection of light verse for children.

BEL.S.V

Sonnets and Verse, by H. BELLOC
Duckworth London 1923 repr. 1947
The adult poetry of one of the best known writers for children.

BET.P

John Betjeman's Collected Poems, comp. EARL OF BIRKENHEAD
Murray London 1958
Witty poems of daily life. Usually too sophisticated for children, but this must be left to the teacher's discretion.

B.L.A.F.S

Best Loved American Folk Songs, collected JOHN and ALAN LOMAX
Grosset and Dunlop New York 1947
Admirable selection for children, taken from F.S.N.A.; invaluable for a teacher. With good, simple piano accompaniments (and guitar chords) by Ruth and Charles Seeger.

BLA.P
Poetry and Prose of William Blake, ed. G. KEYNES
Nonesuch London 1927
> Many *Songs of Innocence* are enjoyed by children; Blake's direct expression can lead children to appreciate, at their own level, poems which they may later understand more fully.

BLA.PENG
A Selection of Poems and Letters of William Blake, ed. J. BRONOWSKI
Penguin 1958
> Includes all a teacher would wish to use.

BL.J
Blackwell's Junior Poetry Books I, II, III, IV, chosen EVAN OWEN
Blackwell 1960 repr. 1964
> A fresh selection, clearly set out and skilfully graded, for the junior school, with much good verse for the youngest children. Great emphasis on rhythm. Disappointing illustrations.

B.P
Birthright Poetry I, II, III, IV, selected W. T. CUNNINGHAM
Hamish Hamilton 1963
> Pleasant selection graded for juniors, and including both traditional and modern verse.

BUN
A Bundle of Ballads, comp. R. MANNING-SANDERS
Oxford University Press 1959
> Well-chosen selection of ballads for schools; tactfully modernized spelling where necessary for easy reading.

CHER
The Cherry Tree, chosen G. GRIGSON
Phoenix House London 1959
> Invaluable for the teacher, and for school and class libraries. Over 500 poems of every imaginable kind, most usefully arranged to enhance each other, in twenty-nine sections. Much not to be found elsewhere. For all ages.

CHES.P

The Collected Poems of G. K. Chesterton

Methuen London 1927 3rd edn. 1933

> Children can enjoy Chesterton's swinging rhythms and his towering fantasy.

CH.GAR

A Child's Garland, gathered JANE CARTON

Faber and Faber 1942 7th imp. 1955

> A selection of fine quality: poetry rather than verse.

C.MUSE

The Common Muse, ed. V. DE SOLA PINTO and A. E. RODWAY

Chatto and Windus London 1957 and Penguin 1965

> Four centuries of ballads and broadsides. The enterprising history teacher could find many useful passages, but there is a great deal of amatory and bawdy verse not suitable for the class-room. Interesting introduction; helpful discography and bibliography.

COM

Common Ground, ed. LEONARD CLARK

Faber and Faber London 1964

> An unusual selection, well-grouped and attractively set out. This anthology would be valuable with top juniors and throughout the secondary school.

COME

Come Hither, made by WALTER DE LA MARE

Constable and Co. London 1923, continually reprinted, new edn. 1960

> 'God's plenty'; almost ideal anthology for those of all ages who enjoy de la Mare's own poetry. Lots of notes 'round and about' the poems, to increase the reader's perception and enjoyment. Boys can find it a little too gentle and sentimental.

C.S.B
The Children's Song Book, ELIZABETH POSTON
Bodley Head London 1961
> Musicianly and delightful, but not too difficult, accompaniments to well-chosen songs which younger children enjoy.

CUM.PENG
e. e. cummings selected poems 1923–58
Penguin (in association Faber) London 1963
> Older children are interested in cummings' typographical experiments and teachers will be able to select several suitable poems.

DAWN
Dawn and Dusk, ed. CHARLES CAUSLEY
Brockhampton Press Ltd. Leicester 1962
> Ninety-one poems by fifty modern poets; unusual, up-to-date choices for older children, made by a schoolmaster-poet who writes an interesting introduction.

DAY
This Day and Age, selected STANLEY HEWETT B.A.
Edward Arnold London 1960
> Poems written since 1919, with a good proportion by American and Commonwealth poets not well-known here. For secondary children.

DE LA M.CH
A Choice of De La Mare's Verse, selected with introd. W. H. AUDEN
Faber Paperback London 1963
> Contains many later poems rarely found in anthologies.

DE LA M.P
Poems 1901–1918, I, II, WALTER DE LA MARE
Constable London 1920 5th imp. 1928
> The poet *par excellence* for gentle and imaginative children. True poetry appears even in his lightest pieces. Selections are available in various paperback editions, Puffin, Pocket Poets, DE LA M.CH.

D.P.F.F
Discovering Poetry IV Fresh Fields
D.P.JOU
Discovering Poetry I The Journey Begins
D.P.ROAD
Discovering Poetry III The Road Ahead
D.P.WAY
Discovering Poetry II The Way Opens,
chosen by E. W. PARKER
Longmans London 1953

>   A popular well-graded series for secondary schools.

DRUM
Drums and Trumpets, selected LEONARD CLARK
The Bodley Head London 1962

>   Snatches from poems of high quality, and some complete
>   poems, for the youngest children; pleasantly grouped by
>   theme.

ECHO
The Echoing Green I, II, III, ed. C. DAY LEWIS
Blackwell Oxford 1937 repr. 1951

>   A deliberately wide selection with immense variety of
>   period, subject and tone. A poet's choice specifically for ages
>   eleven to fourteen, but good for anyone.

EL.O.P
Old Possum's Book of Practical Cats, T. S. ELIOT
Faber London 1939 5th imp. 1943

>   A distinguished modern poet writes for his friends' children.
>   *Skimbleshanks the Railway Cat* (after Kipling) is particularly
>   popular.

EL.P
Collected Poems 1909–1935, T. S. ELIOT
Faber London 1958

>   Teachers may wish to introduce children to lines from one
>   of the greatest twentieth-century poets.

EV.M

Every Man Will Shout, comp. R. MANSFIELD and ed. I. ARMSTRONG
Oxford University Press 1964

Poems on themes which should appeal especially to teen-agers: deliberately 'unpoetic' in manner and style.

EX.T.CH

Exploring Poetry: Treasure Chest

EX.T.H

Exploring Poetry: Treasure Hunt

EX.T.TRA

Exploring Poetry: Treasure Trail

EX.T.TRO

Exploring Poetry: Treasure Trove
ed. E. W. PARKER
Longmans London 1961

Children's poems both traditional and modern, grouped by subject and graded for juniors.

FAB.BAL

The Faber Book of Ballads, ed. MATTHEW HODGART
Faber London 1965

Ballads and broadsides from country and town, mainly useful for older children. Some unusual Australian ballads for tough boys, and some verses from Ireland and America.

FAB.C.V

The Faber Book of Children's Verse, ed. JANET ADAM SMITH
Faber London 1953

Admirably wide-ranging selection, for children already interested in poetry, including many classic poets—Marvell, Milton, Pound. Grouped under imaginative headings: Night and Day, Marvels and Riddles, History and Time. All ages from top juniors upwards.

FAB.M.V

The Faber Book of Modern Verse, ed. M. ROBERTS, suppl. ANNE RIDLER

Faber London new edn. 1960

> A wide-ranging adult anthology for older children to explore.

FAB.N.V

The Faber Book of Nursery Verse, ed. BARBARA IRESON

Faber London 1958

> Splendid collection for younger children—well beyond nursery age—with much that top juniors appreciate. Emphasis on rhythmic verse easy to speak aloud.

F.FEET

Four Feet and Two, comp. LEILA BERG

Puffin London 1960

> Animal poems, including some unusual choices, mainly for juniors.

FIRE.F.S

The Fireside Book of Folk Songs, selected MARGARET BRADFORD BONI

Simon and Schuster New York 1947

> Delightfully illustrated collection of songs from many countries, with helpful accompaniments. In every mood, sacred and profane, gay and sombre. A superb collection for a class teacher.

FLA

Flash Point, comp. ROBERT SHAW

E. J. Arnold London 1964

> Adult poems, mainly modern, chosen to interest top forms. Biographical notes on the poets.

FRO.P

Complete Poems of Robert Frost

Henry Holt and Co. New York 1957

> A wealth of poetry by a major American poet, often simple

enough for juniors while profound enough for adults. His narrative poems are remarkable for their evocations of rural life.

FRO.PENG

Selected Poems, ROBERT FROST
Penguin London 1955
> See **FRO.P**; this is a most useful selection.

FRO.YOU

You Come Too, ROBERT FROST
Bodley Head London 1964
> See **FRO.P**; a splendid selection for children.

F.S.N.A

The Folk Songs of North America, ALAN LOMAX
Cassell London 1960 2nd edn. 1963
> The most comprehensive and authoritative collection, with history of each song and ample accounts of the general background of each group of songs. Invaluable for the school library.

F.Y.D

For Your Delight, ed. ETHEL L. FOWLER
Faber London 1924 republ. 1960
> Pleasant poems; perhaps inclined to sentimentality; mainly for young children.

GOD.JER

St. Jerome and the Lion, RUMER GODDEN
Macmillan London 1961
> Delightful, pleasantly illustrated, retelling of the legend of St. Jerome, for the classroom library.

GRA.FID

The Penny Fiddle: Poems for Children, ROBERT GRAVES
Cassell London 1960
> Twenty-three poems, some of them splendid for children, by a major poet; delightfully illustrated by Ardizzone.

GRA.P
Collected Poems 1959, ROBERT GRAVES
> Children can enjoy several poems and lay a foundation for later reading.

GRA.PENG
Robert Graves: Poems Selected by Himself
Penguin Poets 1957
> See **GRA.P**.

G.TR.P
The Golden Treasury of Poetry, selected LOUIS UNTERMEYER
Collins London 1961
> Valuable collection for all ages—the American format makes it appear to be for younger children. Contains unusual American poems.

GUN.HUG
Selected Poems, THOM GUNN and TED HUGHES
Faber London 1957 repr. 1963
> Adult selection from which a few poems for teenagers can be chosen.

HAP
Happenings: new poems for junior schools, ed. M. WOLLMAN and D. GRUGEON
Harrap London 1964
> Unusual and good poems—many of them suitable for secondary schools also; rather irrelevant photographs chosen to stimulate children's writing.

HAR.PENG
Thomas Hardy, ed. W. E. WILLIAMS
Penguin Poets 1960
> Hardy's poems of the countryside are particularly enjoyed.

HAR.SEL
Selected Poems of Thomas Hardy, ed. P. N. FURBANK
Macmillan London 1964
> Over eighty of Hardy's poems with sensitive introduction.

HERE
Here Today, ed. TED HUGHES
Hutchinson Educational Ltd. London 1963

> A modern poet's modern selection; many poems difficult but rewarding; a few 'sick'. Accompanying records are available: JUR OOA6 and OOA7.

HOU.P
The Collected Poems of A. E. Housman
Cape London 1939

> Poems not as simple as they appear to be; to be used with discretion.

HU.MEET
Meet My Folks, TED HUGHES
Faber London 1961

> Delightful nonsense poems about his sister Jane (a 'big black crow'), his grandfather the 'owler' and other relations. Also on record E.M.I. CLP/1893.

Also

Meet My Folks, music by GORDON CROSSE, poems TED HUGHES
Oxford University Press 1965

> For Speaker, Children's Chorus and Percussion Band and Adult Percussion and Instrument Players.

IRON
Iron, Honey, Gold I, II, ed. DAVID HOLBROOK
Cambridge University Press 1961

> An interesting and individual collection; adolescents quickly appreciate many of the poems, and can be helped to enjoy those that are more difficult. Also obtainable in four books.

IVES
The Burl Ives Song Book
Ballantine New York 1953

> Paperback: excellent value for money; 115 folk songs with notes, guitar chords and piano accompaniment. Difficult to keep open on the piano.

JA.PO
Jazz Poems, selected ANSELM HOLLO
Vista Books Longacre Press London 1963
>   Something new for upper forms.

JOY
The Joy of Life, ed. E. V. LUCAS
Methuen London 1927
>   Forty years old, but full of enjoyable poems for teenagers.

KEY
Poetry One, Two, Three, Four
The Key of the Kingdom, chosen RAYMOND O'MALLEY and DENYS
THOMPSON
Chatto and Windus London 1961, 1961, 1962, 1963
>   An excellent set of class anthologies for secondary children.
>   The non-specialist in particular will be helped by the group-
>   ing together of poems which illuminate each other, or can
>   be fruitfully compared. All moods, periods, styles. Rich
>   collection of very very short poems.

KIP.INC
Rudyard Kipling's Verse, incl. edn. 1885–1932
Hodder and Stoughton 1933
>   A storehouse; much for the historian; poems for all ages,
>   good for saying aloud.

LAW.PENG
Selected Poems of D. H. Lawrence
Penguin 1950 repr. 1960
>   Children enjoy the wonderful animal poems.

LEA.NON
Nonsense Songs, EDWARD LEAR
Vista Books London 1961
>   Cheap and useful collection of favourite nonsense verses.

LIN.P

Collected Poems of Vachel Lindsay

Macmillan New York 1925

> The very unusual jazz rhythms surprise and delight children. Splendid for chanting aloud.

M.CENT

Poems of the Mid-Century, ed. JOHN HOLLOWAY

Harrap London 1957

> Wide variety of poems written after 1940. Chosen to cover everyday subjects and experiences as well as rare ones. For older, abler children; arranged in order of difficulty.

MER

The Merry-Go-Round, chosen JAMES REEVES

Heinemann London 1955 repr. 1956

> Excellent anthology for all juniors, chosen by a poet. Many rhymes, jingles and traditional nursery ballads.

MIL.N.S

Now We Are Six, A. A. MILNE

Methuen London 1927

> Used with discrimination, some of Milne's gay verses can still delight younger children.

M.M.A

Mystery, Magic and Adventure, chosen JOHN A. CUTFORTH

Basil Blackwell, Oxford 1955

> A pleasantly robust collection, splendid for reading aloud. Great diversity; includes admirable extracts from Shakespeare, as well as limericks and music-hall songs.

MOD

Modern Verse 1900–1950, chosen PHYLLIS M. JONES

World's Classics Oxford University Press 1940 2nd edn. 1955 repr. 1959

> Fifth volume of World's Classics anthologies; rather conventional but useful selection of the better known poems of the period. Mainly for older children.

M.P.W

The Modern Poet's World, ed. JAMES REEVES

Heinemann London 1957 repr. 1962

> Complement to *The Poet's World* (P.W.) Adult poems from the first half of the twentieth-century (alphabetically arranged). With notes and introduction on the function of poetry in contemporary life.

M.R.CHA

Mood and Rhythm IV Changes of Mood

M.R.FEEL

Mood and Rhythm I Feeling the Tempo

M.R.HAND

Mood and Rhythm III A Handful of Stars

M.R.ON

Mood and Rhythm II On the Beat

Chosen by ESMÉ MEARS

A. & C. Black London 1963

> Very well-indexed selections; titles explanatory.

MY

My Kind of Verse, comp. JOHN SMITH

Burke London 1965

> A Junior School Anthology containing the poems selected by the English Speaking Board for their examinations. Gentle, even a little sentimental, in general tone, but contains a variety of both familiar and unusual verse good for speaking aloud.

NA.P.B

The Pocket Book of Ogden Nash, introd. L. UNTERMEYER

Pocket Books Inc. N.Y. 1962

> Excellent selection from leading American humorist with absolutely idiosyncratic style and wit.

NA.P.D.R
The Private Dining Room, ODGEN NASH
Dent London 1953
   See **NA.P.B**

OWEN.P
Collected Poems of Wilfred Owen, ed. C. DAY LEWIS
Chatto and Windus London 1963
   Owen is the poet of World War I who seems to appeal most
   deeply to modern adolescents.

OX.E.V
The Oxford Book of English Verse
Oxford University Press
   A standard anthology: good reference book for better-
   known English poems throughout the centuries.

OX.L.V
The Oxford Book of Light Verse, chosen W. H. AUDEN
Oxford University Press 1938 repr. 1939
   Many serious, but no solemn, verses of various periods—
   many ballads old and new. A valuable collection for the
   teacher.

OX:N.R
The Oxford Nursery Rhyme Book, ed. I. and P. OPIE
Oxford University Press 1955 repr. 1963
   The most complete collection available—invaluable for
   teachers of the youngest children.

OX.P.C
The Oxford Book of Poetry for Children, ed. E. BLISHEN
Oxford University Press 1963
   Beautifully produced; illustrated by Brian Wildsmith. An
   excellent choice of real poems, designed for younger
   children but appropriate at many ages. Should be in every
   class library.

OX.S.M.J
Oxford School Music Books: Junior I, II, III

OX.S.M.P
Oxford School Music Books: Preliminary Book

OX.S.M.S
Oxford School Music Books: Senior I, II, III
ROGER FISKE and J. P. B. DOBBS
Oxford University Press 1954 and 1956
> Delightful variety of songs and recorder music in preliminary book, then most useful courses both junior and senior. Songs from many countries, in different styles and moods, and introductions to some instruments.

OX.V.J
The Oxford Books of Verse for Juniors I, II, III, IV, ed. JAMES BRITTON
Oxford University Press 1957 repr. 1958
> Admirable for class use: attractively printed poems (often modern) including many not to be found elsewhere.

PAT
The Pattern of Poetry, ed. W. K. SEYMOUR and J. SMITH
Burke Publishing Co. Ltd. London 1963
> Specially good for reading aloud from, because poems are those chosen for the verse speaking examinations of the Poetry Society. Ranges over four centuries, and is meant for all ages.

PEG
Pegasus I, II, III, IV, V, ed. N. GRISENTHWAITE
Schofield and Sims Ltd. Huddersfield 1962
> An excellent, lively collection for use as secondary class books, carefully graded, and with some unexpected choices.

PEL.AN

An Anthology of Animal Poetry, ed. K. A. MASON
Pelican 1940

> Unfortunately out of print, but an admirable collection worth trying to pick up second-hand. To some extent replaced by **PENG.AN**

PENG.A.F.S

The Penguin Book of American Folk Songs, ed. ALAN LOMAX
Penguin 1964 reset in improved format 1965

> Admirable collection by a real authority, with helpful notes on each song, piano accompaniments, and some good instructions for learning the guitar. Discography.

PENG.AN

The Penguin Book of Animal Verse, introd. and ed. GEORGE MACBETH
Penguin 1965

> Poems on animals, alphabetically arranged, in widest variety of style, mood, period and sophistication. Some complete poems, and parts of many others, will delight children.

PENG.C.A.P

Contemporary American Poetry, selected DONALD HALL
Penguin 1962

> Adult anthology in which a teacher can find some new poems for older children.

PENG.COM

The Penguin Book of Comic and Curious Verse, coll. J. M. COHEN
Penguin 1952 repr. 1958

> With **PENG.M.C** and **PENG.YET**, three volumes of all kinds of light and humorous verse, from which occasional gems can be plucked.

PENG.C.V

The Penguin Book of Contemporary Verse, ed. K. ALLOTT
Penguin 1950 2nd edn. 1962

> Poems written over the last fifty years, many of which

appeal to older children. For the academic adolescent, a book
to browse in. The teacher will find useful biographical notes
on each poet.

PENG.E.V
The Penguin Book of English Verse, ed. JOHN HAYWARD
Penguin 1956

Intelligently and sensitively chosen samples of great English
poets, from Wyatt to Dylan Thomas.

PENG.M.A.V
The Penguin Book of Modern American Verse, selected GEOFFREY
MOORE
Penguin 1954

Useful discussion of each poet; a collection from which the
teacher can choose fresh poems for older children.

PENG.M.C
More Comic and Curious Verse, coll. J. M. COHEN
Penguin 1956 repr. 1958

See **PENG.COM**

PENG.NEW
New Poetry, selected A. ALVAREZ
Penguin 1962

Gives the teacher an opportunity to introduce really modern
poetry to top forms.

PENG.YET
Yet More Comic and Curious Verse, selected J. M. COHEN
Penguin 1959 repr. 1964

See **PENG.COM**

P.F.P
Poems for Pleasure I, II, ed. A. F. SCOTT
Cambridge University Press 1955

Very well arranged under such headings as Rhythm in Verse
or Scenes of the Machine Age, this selection is useful from
top juniors to adults. A third book advises the teacher on
presentation of the poems.

P.LIFE

Poetry and Life I, II, III, IV, ed. N. GRISENTHWAITE
Schofield and Sims Ltd. Huddersfield 1961

> Poems both attractive to children and of real quality. One of the best sets for the junior classroom; much traditional material attractive to the ear.

P.P.BELL

Poetry for Pleasure II Bells Across the Sand, 1952

P.P.BRA

Poetry for Pleasure VI The Brave Days of Old, 1959

P.P.FACT

Poetry for Pleasure III Facts and Fancies, 1952

P.P.FAL

Poetry for Pleasure VII Falling Splendours, 1959

P.P.OVER

Poetry for Pleasure V Over the Hill, 1958

P.P.SAL

Poetry for Pleasure I Sally Go Round the Moon, 1952

P.P.TALK

Poetry for Pleasure IV Talk and Tale, 1952

P.P.WIDE

Poetry for Pleasure VIII The Wide World's End, 1960
Chosen IAN PARSONS
Ginn London

> Eight admirable graded volumes; the first two rich in memorable jingles; the selection widens and deepens with each volume.

P.REM

Poems to Remember, comp. PATRIC DICKINSON and SHEILA SHANNON
Harvil Press London 1958

> Some good poems for secondary schools.

P.SING

The Poet Sings, selected A. D. DODD and C. I. FAULDING
Juta & Co. Capetown n.d.

> Admirable selection for ages thirteen and over, with a section of poems on South Africa by South Africans.

P.TIME

Poems of Our Time 1900–1942, chosen R. CHURCH and M. M. BOZMAN
Dent Everyman London 1945

> Interesting selection; a carefully chosen group of war poems of 1914–18 suitable for older boys.

P.TONG

The Poet's Tongue I, II, ed. W. H. AUDEN and GARRATT
Bell London 1935

> First-rate book for the teacher; poems for all ages. Lots of traditional verse in varied moods for both lowbrows and highbrows, as well as suitable poems by Donne, Milton and Shakespeare.

PUF.N.R

Puffin Book of Nursery Rhymes, ed. I. and P. OPIE
Penguin 1963

> Selected from **OX.N.R**, an admirable collection for the youngest children, very attractively presented.

PUF.Q

A Puffin Quartet of Poets, ELEANOR FARJEON, JAMES REEVES, E. V. RIEU, IAN SERRAILLIER
Penguin 1958

> Delightful new poems by four authors who excel in writing for children.

PUF.V

Puffin Book of Verse, ed. E. GRAHAM
Penguin 1953 repr. 1962

> A rather conventional, but wide, selection, which children can explore.

P.W
The Poet's World, ed. JAMES REEVES
Heinemann 1948 reset 1963
> A poet's selection from a thousand years of English poetry, including particularly well-chosen passages from the Old Testament.

REE.P.A
Prefabulous Animiles, JAMES REEVES and EDWARD ARDIZZONE
Heinemann 1957 repr. 1961
> Comic animals—the Hippocrump, the Nimp and others—described and pictured in a way most attractive to juniors.

REE.W.M
The Wandering Moon, JAMES REEVES
Heinemann London 1950 new edn. 1957
> One of the modern poets most appreciated by younger children.

RIS
Rising Early, ed. CHARLES CAUSLEY
Brockhampton Press Ltd. Leicester 1964
> A poet's choice of twentieth-century story poems and ballads, for older children. Some have a slightly sick flavour.

R.R
Rhyme and Reason, chosen R. O'MALLEY and D. THOMPSON
Chatto and Windus London 1957
> For the oldest children, a particularly good selection of 175 sensitively chosen poems of every period and style, grouped by subject. Interesting introduction and really close consideration of text in helpful notes.

SCH.M.V
The School Book of Modern Verse, chosen GUY BOAS
Macmillan London 1962
> A selection for older, academic children.

SER.HAP
Happily Ever After, IAN SERRAILLIER
Oxford University Press 1963
> A slim volume of new poems by a modern poet who appeals to the imagination of children. Good illustrations by Wildsmith.

S.N.W
Songs of the New World, ed. DESMOND MACMAHON
McDougall's Educational Co. Edinburgh n.d.
> Thirty-four popular American folk-songs with simple piano accompaniment and guitar chords.

SPIR
Poems of Spirit and Action, selected W. M. SMYTH
Edward Arnold 1957 repr. 1960
> Vigorous, straightforward poems, mainly narrative, popular with younger secondary children.

S.T.S
Something to Sing I, II, comp. GEOFFREY BRACE
Cambridge University Press 1963 and 1965
> Very varied collection, from folk-song to opera, Victorian music hall to Mozart, with bibliographies of songs and records.

THEME
Theme and Variations, selected R. B. HEATH
Longmans 1965
> For older children. Thought-provoking poems on God, Nature and Man. With suggestions for further reading and useful bibliographies.

THIS.W.D
This Way Delight, selected HERBERT READ
Faber London 1957
Poems mainly lyrical and fantastical. Some unexpected modern
> poets.

THO.GR

The Green Roads, poems by EDWARD THOMAS, chosen and introd.
ELEANOR FARJEON
Bodley Head London 1965
> Admirable selection for secondary schools, with charming introduction by a personal friend of the poet's, telling how Thomas began to write.

THO.SEL

Selected Poems of Edward Thomas, ed. R. S. THOMAS
Faber London 1964
> Mainly adult poems, but the teacher can find many short passages on natural scenes which children enjoy and appreciate.

TODAY

Poems of Today 1st and *2nd series*
Sidgwick and Jackson 1927
> Famous Georgian collections: many of the poems appeal to children by their simplicity and directness.

TOM.T.G

Tom Tiddler's Ground, chosen W. DE LA MARE
Bodley Head London 1931 new edn. 1961
> A sensitively chosen cross-section of English poetry for imaginative children, with really illuminating notes. All ages.

TREE

The Tree in the Wood I The Egg in the Nest
The Tree in the Wood II The Nest on the Twig
The Tree in the Wood III The Twig on the Bough
The Tree in the Wood IV The Bough on the Tree
A Junior Anthology chosen by RAYMOND O'MALLEY and DENYS THOMPSON
Chatto and Windus London 1966
> Outstandingly good junior series, beautifully set out for easy reading. Wide variety of poems of quality, each good of its kind, grave or gay, homely or fantastic, sense or nonsense.

TW.N

Twentieth Century Narrative Poems, ed. M. WOLLMAN

Harrap 1954 repr. 1957

Thirty-five modern narrative poems in varying moods, for abler, older children.

UNDER

Modern Poems Understood, ed. C. W. GILLAM

Harrap London 1965

Poems written from 1914 to 1964: a really useful secondary selection. Notes a little trite.

V.F

Verse That Is Fun, selected BARBARA IRESON

Faber and Faber London 1962

Humorous poems and jingles, long and short, credited and anonymous. Almost everyone could find something here for occasional light relief.

WAL.C.P

Chinese Poems, trans. ARTHUR WALEY

Allen and Unwin 1946 4th imp. 1962

Admirable as English poems in their own right. Also most useful for showing both that poetry need not rhyme, and that the same problems have faced people for a very long time.

WEALTH

A Wealth of Poetry, comp. WINIFRED HINDLEY and JOHN BETJEMAN

Blackwell Oxford 1963

An anthology of high quality. Over 250 poems, many of them very popular with children, and over a quarter by living poets. Arranged by theme, they cover a wide range of emotions. Dazzling abstract decorations.

WHEEL

The Wheel of Poetry, *I*, *II*, *III*, *IV*, comp. JEROME HANRATTY
University of London Press 1963

> For secondary pupils; chronologically arranged in each volume, but useful suggestions for grouping are given, and a few helpful notes.

W.S.O

We Shall Overcome, comp. GUY and CANDIE CARAWAN
Oak Publications New York 1963

> Songs which are being sung in the struggle for integration in the United States. Explanations of their use and provenance are given, and accounts of the effect when sung in and out of prison.

Y.B.S

A Year Book of the Stars, legends retold by CHRISTINE CHAUNDLER
Mowbray and Co. London 1956

> Not a poetry book: included for the Zodiac rhyme not available elsewhere.

YEA.P

The Collected Poems of W. B. Yeats
Macmillan London 1950

> A very great poet, some of whose poems can well be introduced to older children.

YOU.P

The Collected Poems of Andrew Young, arranged L. CLARK
Hart-Davies London 1960

> Distinguished modern nature poet. For children, the descriptive parts of his poems are admirable, and should be used by themselves.

RECORDED POETRY

As well as the records noted above, and records on which individual poets speak their own poems, the following may be of use:

Anthology of Ballads, JUR 00A3
The Barrow Poets, RG 360
Caedmon Treasury of Modern Poets, TCO 994
Junior Anthology of English Verse, JUR 00B1, 00B3, 00B5
Jupiter Anthology of Twentieth-Century Poetry, JUR 00A1
Pattern of Poetry (in eight parts), CLP 1724, etc.
Rhyme and Reason, ZRG 5414–7, RG 417